SELF-ESTEEM FOR BEGINNERS

2 Books in 1: Conquer Anxiety, Improve Your Social Skills, Realize Your Value, Increase Self-Confidence and Overcome Shyness

Elizabeth Wright

© Copyright 2020 by Elizabeth Wright. All rights reserved.

The material contained herein is presented with the intent of furnishing pertinent and relevant information and knowledge on the topic with the sole purpose of providing entertainment. The author should thus not be considered an expert on the topic in this material despite any claims to such expertise, first-hand knowledge and any other reasonable claim to specific knowledge on the material contained herein. The information presented in this work has been researched to ensure its reasonable accuracy and validity. Nevertheless, it is advisable to consult with a duly licensed professional in the area pertaining to this topic, or any other covered in this book, in order to ensure the quality and validity of the advice and/or techniques contained in this material.

This is a legally binding statement as deemed so by the Committee of Publishers Association and the American Bar Association in the United States. Any reproduction, transmission, copying or otherwise duplication of the material contained in this work are in violation of current copyright legislation. No physical or digital copies of this work, both total and partial, may not be done without the Publisher's express written consent. All additional rights are reserved by the publisher of this work.

The data, facts and description of events forthwith shall be considered as accurate unless the work is deemed to be a work of fiction. In any event, the Publisher is exempt of responsibility for any use of the information contained in the present work on the part of the user. The author and Publisher may not be deemed liable, under any circumstances, for the events resulting from the observance of the advice, tips, techniques and any other contents presented herein.

Given the informational and entertainment nature of the content presented in this work, there is no guarantee as to the quality and validity of the information. As such, the contents of this work are deemed as universal. No use of copyrighted material is used in this work. Any references to other trademarks are done so under fair use and by no means represent an endorsement of such trademarks or their holder.

TABLE OF CONTENTS

SELF-ESTEEM FOR BEGINNERS

Conquer Anxiety, Overcome Shyness, Improve Your People Skills, Boost Your Self-Confidence and Take Control of Your Life

Elizabeth Wright

© Copyright 2020 by Elizabeth Wright
All rights reserved.
The material contained herein is presented with the intent of furnishing pertinent and relevant information and knowledge on the topic with the sole purpose of providing entertainment. The author should thus not be considered an expert on the topic in this material despite any claims to such expertise, first-hand knowledge and any other reasonable claim to specific knowledge on the material contained herein. The information presented in this work has been researched to ensure its reasonable accuracy and validity. Nevertheless, it is advisable to consult with a duly licensed professional in the area pertaining to this topic, or any other covered in this book, in order to ensure the quality and validity of the advice and/or techniques contained in this material.
This is a legally binding statement as deemed so by the Committee of Publishers Association and the American Bar Association in the United States. Any reproduction, transmission, copying or otherwise duplication of the material contained in this work are in violation of current copyright legislation. No physical or digital copies of this work, both total and partial, may not be done without the Publisher's express written consent. All additional rights are reserved by the publisher of this work.
The data, facts and description of events forthwith shall be considered as accurate unless the work is deemed to be a work of fiction. In any event, the Publisher is exempt of responsibility for any use of the information contained in the present work on the part of the user. The author and Publisher may not be deemed liable, under any circumstances, for the events resulting from the observance of the advice, tips, techniques and any other contents presented herein.
Given the informational and entertainment nature of the content presented in this work, there is no guarantee as to the quality and validity of the information. As such, the contents of this work are deemed as universal. No use of copyrighted material is used in this work. Any references to other trademarks are done so under fair use and by no means represent an endorsement of such trademarks or their holder.

INTRODUCTION

Thanks for purchasing *Self-Esteem for Beginners*. By purchasing this book, you can begin a journey of improving your self-esteem and allowing yourself to go through life with more confidence and less self-doubt. Using scientific and psychological research, I will show you what self-esteem is, and how your brain processes messages of self-doubt. You will learn just a little bit of the neuroscience that drives self-esteem so you can address your problem areas. While some complex areas will be covered, it is all written in straightforward ways that anyone can understand and enjoy! This book will show you how to put your doubts behind you and walk into the future, and it uses examples of real people who have changed their lives using these methods.

In this book, you will learn not only about what self-esteem is, but you will learn why you don't have it and how to address it. Too many people live their lives feeling unworthy. They don't believe in themselves, and because they don't believe in themselves, they can never accomplish the results that they want. It takes time to improve your self-esteem, and you'll have to fight for the results you want, but with the guidance of your book, you can start improving your self-esteem today.

Many books handle this same topic, so I appreciate you choosing this one and assure that I have done everything possible to include information that will be the most helpful to you. Enjoy this book! The lessons taught here should last long after you close this book, and they should drive your future. I hope that you can change your life for the better and develop some self-esteem. You deserve it!

CHAPTER 1
What Is Self-Esteem

What It Means to Have Self-Esteem

In short, self-esteem is how you feel about yourself. It is the sum of the worth you feel about yourself. It includes a wide range of factors about yourself including your body, your mind, your values, your feelings, and your actions. Self-esteem is the way you judge who you are, and when you have self-esteem, you judge yourself positively and believe that you have worth as a person. There are varying levels of self-esteem, and some people may be confident in one area of their life while feeling insecure in another. Some people have self-esteem that is low in all or most areas of their lives, and that level of self-esteem is debilitating.

Those with self-esteem will fight for their interests and be unafraid of their own opinions. People who have self-esteem think that their beliefs are worth going to bat for. People with low self-esteem may assume that their interests are somehow shameful or that they are always wrong. When you have self-esteem, you can take risks without feeling like you're bound for failure. People who have self-esteem know that risk comes with rewards while people who don't have self-esteem may be holding themselves back. Stop holding yourself back, and let the transformative power of self-esteem have a special part in your life so you can stand up for yourself and your interests.

When you have self-esteem, you trust yourself. You know that you'll do the right thing, You don't second guess what your values are. You don't let anyone convince you that you are wrong without some analysis. Whereas people without self-esteem may assume that they are wrong when challenged, people with self-esteem can take a more analytical approach. They can accept a challenge without losing their identities or feeling like they are worthless. People with self-esteem can admit that they are wrong because they trust themselves to know when to stand by their opinions and when to reevaluate based on doubts. Confidence, therefore, isn't about never being wrong. It is about trusting that you'll find what is right.

People with self-esteem feel confident. Confidence is one of the best feelings that comes with self-esteem. People with self-esteem feel as though they can take on the world and whatever challenges it brings. They feel good in their own skins, and they don't worry that there is something inherently wrong with them. When you have confidence, life is a lot sunnier, and when it becomes cloudy, you don't break down under pressure. You're able to weather storms that come your way, and you can accept that even during the bad times, you're still overall a self-assured person.

People with self-esteem feel worthy. When you have self-esteem, you are worth it. You are worth happiness. You are worth a promotion. You are worth your family and friends. You are worth all the good things that happen to you, and your worth doesn't disappear the second you make a mistake. We all have worth, but people who don't have self-esteem often lose sight of their worth. They can't get in touch with the things that make them feel worthy, which causes them to lose a big chunk of themselves. Many experiences can make people feel unworthy, but self-esteem brings that worth back.

If you have self-esteem, you believe that you can handle problems. You don't become chicken little and fear that the sky is going to fall after any mild obstacle. You're able to take a step back, breathe, and remember that you have the skills to do what you need to do to fix whatever mess you've wound up in. When you have self-esteem, problem-solving comes more easily because you can focus on your skills rather than what you can't do.

Self-esteem allows you to have strong, mutually respectful relationships. When you have self-esteem, you can make sure that people in your life treat you with the respect that you deserve. When you have low self-esteem, it's too easy to let people who are no good for you to dominate your life. People in abusive or toxic relationships often end up with low self-esteem, which makes it harder to get out of hard relationships. It's hard to keep control of your relationships when you feel that you don't deserve better than you already have. Thus, self-esteem ensures that you have a good relationship.

Self-esteem includes all parts of yourself— body, mind, and soul. It makes up who you are, and if you aren't comfortable with who you are, you'll never be able to use self-esteem to your advantage. Self-esteem means that you believe that all those parts of you can combine and work together to keep you healthy and happy. If you are lacking in self-esteem in one of these areas, or all of them, it will be hard to keep up your confidence in the other ones as well. Accordingly, the more you can build your self-esteem, the more positive impacts you'll have in your life.

Do You Lack Self-Esteem?

The following are some questions you can ask yourself to see if you lack self-esteem. If your answer to any of the following is yes, then you probably have at least minor self-confidence issues. The more you say yes to the questions, the more your lack of self-esteem impacts your life. It's crucial to be honest with yourself about your answers to these questions. If you can't be honest about your answers, then you are never going to get better. There's no sense in denying how you feel, and there's no shame in feeling that way.

Do you feel as though you can do nothing right? If you feel like there's no way that you can ever do anything right, that suggests that you are looking at yourself with an infinitely negative lens. This kind of negativity only happens when you lack the confidence you need to believe that you can master certain skills and abilities. Perfectionism is rooted in low self-esteem when you think that you can't do anything right because when you need to be perfect, it is because you feel that if you do that then you can finally feel good about yourself. Unfortunately, self-esteem doesn't work that way. You don't feel better about yourself ever because being perfect is impossible.

Are your doubts making it hard to get anything accomplished? Many people who have self-esteem issues have trouble completing tasks or advancing through the ranks of their professional or personal endeavors. Doubt can make you not want to try new things. It can impede you from taking chances that would help you grow as a person. Self-esteem is a problem if it's stopping you from making your dreams a reality.

Does your sense of self-worth depend on achievements? Too many people use achievements to determine whether they are worthy, but achievements don't correlate to your worth. Having ten trophies doesn't make you inherently worth more than having none. Being a millionaire versus living paycheck to paycheck again doesn't make you worth more or less. Your worth should be based on who you are as a whole person. By putting all the weight of your self-worth into one area, you are doing a disservice to yourself because you are not allowing yourself to view yourself as a whole person. You are reducing who you are to something that on its own doesn't matter.

Are you so caught up in success that you lose track of the journey to success? It's easy to get so focused on the end results that those become all that excites you. Just like relying on achievements for your self-worth is erroneous, so is only appreciating the achievements. Enjoy the journey because it is that journey that will give you long-lasting self-esteem. Let's say that you like to knit. What makes you more proud? The fact that you have an end product or all the work and effort you put into making that product. For most people, it is the work. We're proud of the end product because we invested the time, energy, and skill into whatever we were doing.

Is it hard for you to function without feeling like there's something inherently wrong with you? When you have low self-esteem, you're prone to thinking that there's something inherently wrong with you. You think there's a glitch in your DNA that is irreversible and irreparable. You are not broken. You are not a lost cause. Whatever you think is so wrong with you, it's probably something that you can address and improve upon. No matter your past, you can look forward and create a better life for yourself. If you're having trouble accepting that you're not inherently wrong with you, try repeating the words, "I am a whole person, and there is nothing wrong with me that I can't make better."

When you have hardship in your life, do you automatically blame yourself? Not everything is in your power. Sometimes bad things happen, and they aren't your fault. Some things are your fault, but you can't blame yourself for everything, especially things that have been caused by other people who try to convince you that you are the problem. Just like there is not something inherently wrong with you, not everything can be blamed on you. Take responsibility for what you do wrong, but it doesn't help you to be guilty of things that aren't in your power.

Do you hate yourself? Ask yourself if you hate yourself. Do you despise yourself simply for existing? Do you feel bitterness and dread when you look in the mirror? Self-hate is one of the biggest markers of low self-esteem, and it is one of the most painful. When you hate yourself, it is hard to go through life with an open heart and an open mind. It's also hard to ever feel successful. If you hate yourself, you never feel any reward. There's always something left to be unsatisfied about.

Do you treat yourself with anger rather than compassion? When you have low self-esteem, you become your own worst enemy. You start to treat yourself with rage instead of love. You demean yourself for any minor infractions, and you expect more than you can ever accomplish. Instead of being forgiving with yourself, you're nasty. If you wouldn't treat someone you love as you treat yourself then you are probably treating yourself with too little respect. Don't hold yourself to such a high standard and be merciful when you make mistakes because that's the mindset you need to have confidence.

Do you frequently use negative languages about yourself in response to ordinary mistakes? Using negative language against yourself only decreases your self-esteem. Saying things like, "I am ugly," "I am dumb," or "I can't do anything right," are some examples of negative language. This language doesn't do anything constructive for you, so it doesn't help make you any better. Thus, it only serves to decrease your self-esteem. Try swapping out positive language for the negative words. Thus, instead of saying, "I have a big stomach," try saying something like "I like my curves." Find good things to emphasize about yourself rather than all the bad things that your low self-esteem tells you are wrong.

It's common for people who lack self-esteem to show the above markers, along with some others, but you don't have to continue to let these tendencies interfere with your life. Even if you don't want to admit it, low self-esteem makes a huge impact on your ability to function.

How Low Self-Esteem Impacts Your Life

People with low self-esteem don't just feel bad about themselves. Their feelings of inferiority spread. Their low self-esteem impacts every area of their life until they are unable to do anything without their insecurities looming over them. Many people let their doubts control their life. They become driven by their low self-esteem rather than their passions. No matter what you want to do, you aren't going to be able to do it if you don't have self-esteem because you can't be motivated to do anything if you don't even believe in yourself.

They are less able to live their lives. Low self-esteem makes it hard to maintain relationships. People who have low self-esteem can often project their doubts onto their partners or other people in their lives. When you feel bad about yourself, you might start to think that people are bound to leave you even if they have no reason to do so. You think that they'll find a better friend or partner. You feel replaceable, and that causes you to act in ways that may destroy your relationship. You'll either start to pull away, or you will cling onto that relationship, trying to ensure that you won't be left. Insecurities make you think that you have to act in extreme ways to be loved. You may also go to extreme measures to keep relationships that would be healthiest to let go of.

It is also harder to have a fulfilling career when you have low self-esteem because you don't have the confidence to go for promotions or expand your life. I used to have this exact problem. Ten years ago, I would have never written this book. I would have thought, "I am no James Joyce, so I might as well not even try to write." I would belittle my skills and back away from them instead of working to grow as a writer. Logically, I knew all there was to know about self-esteem. I'd read the books and done all the research. I could tell other people how to improve their self-esteem, but in my personal life, I still struggled. My career blossomed when I finally used my own knowledge to start advancing my professional life.

If you have so many negative feelings towards yourself, you may also have trouble making peace with your body. You'll never like what you look like if you don't appreciate your body for what it is. Women especially struggle to have self-esteem as it relates to their bodies. At the age of nine, psychologists like Robin Goodman say that girls' self-esteem plummets. At nine, three-fourths of girls like the way they look, but by twelve that number drops to fifty-six percent. Bodily dissatisfaction continues to increase through high school. Further, by nine at least fifty percent of girls have been on diet. By eighth grade, eighty percent have been on diets. Thus, the bodily focus in our society is well established. One study that shows young children pictures of kids with different bodies— overweight, disfigured, disabled— showed that children responded most negatively to overweight kids. Thus, our society has a huge weight bias, which puts undue pressure on people to have perfect body types even though people have different body types that all can't match the ideal. Knowing these societal factors can help you make sense of the insecurities that you feel rather than blaming yourself for why your body won't do what you want it to.

It's hard to ever feel truly happy when you have low self-esteem. You can have moments of happiness when you have low self-esteem, but those moments will always be muted by all the moments when you feel awful about yourself. Low self-esteem means that it will always be hard for you to catch your breath. You'll always feel like you're huffing and puffing through a race that you can never win. It's an awful feeling that makes you feel drained rather than energized.

Further, people with low self-esteem are more likely to have mental illnesses, which only increases their negative feelings. When you have low self-esteem, the world becomes a dark place, which can make it easier to sink into a deep depression, or you may feel more anxious. If you aren't able to have faith in yourself, it is hard to have faith in the rest of the world. You become more jaded, and you struggle to see the light at the end of the tunnel through all the fog that clouds your vision.

The longer you have low self-esteem, the less confidence you will feel until you make a change. Your self-esteem won't ever get better if you don't address it head-on. You can't hope for it to go away just because good things happen to you. Good things will make you feel temporarily better, but if you don't look at the source of your insecurity, it will fester. It will eat you alive until you don't feel good about anything. You may be able to manage your low self-esteem and act like you're okay, but you will have to make sacrifices because of your low self-esteem.

When you don't have confidence, you don't take charge of your life. You allow people to treat you the same way they always have, even if they treat you the wrong way. You become unable to resist the bad treatment you get because you don't feel like you are worth respect. Thus, it becomes easy for you to disregard your own boundaries. People can more easily take advantage of you and do things that make you feel uncomfortable because you lose track of what is too far. Boundaries are hard to maintain when you aren't consistent with yourself about what you deserve.

Additionally, you will never feel worthy of the good things in your life until you address your low self-esteem. When you have low self-esteem, your whole life is going to suffer, which is why it's so important to change your life now and get rid of lingering self-esteem issues.

Low self-worth causes a variety of issues, and these issues can hit people in different ways. Throughout this book, I will provide case studies of people I've helped who have changed their lives using the techniques in this book. These people show how much self-esteem issues influence normal people's lies, but they also show how there is hope to improve and grow. The first story I'll tell if of a woman named Janet who struggled for years before healing her relationship with herself.

Janet: A Case Study

Janet was a colleague of mine who matched all the markers of low self-esteem. She constantly doubted herself. She tended to keep to herself, and she didn't like to share her opinions. She didn't think she was worthy of the good things that happened to her. She thought that there was something fundamentally wrong with her that could never be fixed. Janet was sure that she was never going to amount to anything despite having a successful career in marketing and raising wonderful kids. Janet constantly dismissed her own skills and her own power to do great things, and in the process, she became stagnated. Her life was spinning in place, and she wanted a change, but with her low self-esteem, she couldn't create that change no matter how hard she tried. She was stuck, and she needed to build her self-esteem to jumpstart her life.

She grew up in a toxic family. Her mother was emotionally abusive, and she would criticize Janet on her weight, and her looks especially, but she would criticize her on most things. Her father was mostly absent. He worked long hours, and when he wasn't working, he'd spend more time drinking with friends than with his family. Janet said that he wasn't an alcoholic but that he overdid it sometimes. He wasn't abusive, but his inattentiveness to his family was felt. Janet's parents commonly fought about money and her father's lack of attention to his wife and kids. Her parents weren't villainous people, but their faults hurt Janet, and sometimes she said that she didn't feel like she existed. As a child, it seemed that no one cared, which added to her feelings of inadequacy as she grew older.

When she was a teen, Janet started expecting more of herself. She wanted to impress her parents because she thought that if she did that she could get their attention, but no matter how hard she tried, they didn't seem to notice. She got all A's, and she was an excellent violinist, but her success never made her feel better about herself. Her success never amounted to any reward from her parents, who were struggling to make the best of things and fighting more often. She hoped that one day she'd be enough to be seen past the dysfunction of her family.

As a perfectionist who wanted to please her family, Janet often did remarkable things, but she didn't feel remarkable. She was second in her high school class, and she graduated from a top college summa cum laude. Yet, nothing was good enough for her to feel self-assured. She was doing well, but she still wondered if she was really just a failure pretending to be successful. People would applaud Janet for her work, but she was constantly doubting their words. She was sure that she could do better and that she had to do better if she wanted to be worth anything. When she went to college, she experienced more hardship that was worsened by the doubts she already had about herself. She began to restrict her eating, which culminated in her eventually developing bulimia. She became consumed with what she ate, and she'd end up eating thousands of calories of food, and she would throw it all up when the feeling of self-loathing hit her. What started as a diet wreaked havoc on her body. She was sick, and her body wasn't working properly. She lost some weight, but again, she didn't feel any better about herself. So many doubts still consumed her mind, and her disorder was just a distraction from her real problems. She continued to be impressive, and she hid the dysfunction from everyone in her life.

She got her eating disorder under control, at least for a little while, after undergrad, and then she went on to grad school. The thought about being too fat and ugly remained, but she was trying to be better. Unfortunately, she still felt insecure. Her insecurities just took other forms. All the things that bothered her about herself before bothered herself now only she had additional insecurities that she piled on top of others. Janet had always been a good student, but grad school was harder, and it was more intense than she expected it to be. She felt overwhelmed by the classwork and didn't feel as smart as her classmates. They were all from impressive schools, and she was from a small liberal arts school. She graduated, again doing well, and was ready to start her career, but she was on edge with the thought that everything was going to tumble off track.

After she had her masters in marketing, Janet entered the workforce to get her first "real" job, and she suffered from imposter syndrome basically from the start. She was sure that she wasn't qualified for her job, even though she was one of the most qualified people in her workplace. She thought that she was faking being smart and that her coworkers would realize that she was just a fraud soon. It didn't matter how well she did on assignments; she felt like she'd never have the success and confidence that she craved. She hoped that someday her work life would give her what she wanted.

Her new job was exciting, but she wasn't ready for the business of it. There were no report cards, so it was harder for her to figure out if she was doing well or not. She needed to know that she was doing well, but it felt like the only feedback she got was criticism. Her boss was a gruff guy who wasn't one for pleasantries. He could come off rude or even mean without meaning to be, so his demeanor made it hard for Janet to know where she stood. She was certain that if there as a report card for her job that she would be getting D's. Since she wasn't fired, she assumed she had to be doing *something* right.

At twenty-five, still feeling like she wasn't good enough for her job, Janet got married to a man who belittled her and repeated many of the unfortunate circumstances of her childhood. He knew exactly where to poke to make Janet upset. He knew about her issues with food, so he made her feel like she took up too much space. He scolded her when she ate too much food or when she gained weight, he'd pinch her stomach and ask her "What's that?" She tried not to let her food issue return, but she slipped up sometimes. Mostly, she was able to keep herself from engaging in too many disordered behaviors by reminding herself that she wanted to start a family. She was sure that having a baby would finally give her the purpose she craved, but that didn't go to plan.

Her life began to crumble even further when she gave birth to her first son, who she loved as much as she hoped she would, but being a new mother wasn't easy. With postpartum depression crippling her, her career not going the way she wanted, her marriage falling apart, and her eating disorder popping up again when she couldn't lose the baby weight, Janet was in a worse position than she ever was. She felt like nothing was going right in her life, which made her feel like she was in a deep, dark hole that she could never get out of.

Janet's marriage ended up in divorce, but not before she had two more children with her soon to be ex-husband. The marriage was long and painful for Janet. Her husband made her self-esteem plummet, and she tried to keep the toxicity of her husband away from her children, but sometimes he would insult them as well, and Janet hated to think what that would do to them as they grew up. She knew she needed to get out, but she feared that she would never be able to stand on her own two feet. Her husband convinced her that she needed him. He would repeat that she wouldn't amount to anything if she was on her own, and to some extent, Janet believed him. She was the moneymaker in the family, but he made her feel like she did nothing for the household.

She adored having her children, but even by the time she had her last child, she still didn't feel like she knew how to be a mother. Every time her newborn cried, she felt like she was failing her. Logically, she knew that wasn't true, but she hated the thought that she wouldn't be the mother her children deserved. She tried to give them everything, but she knew that her husband was a source of negativity in their family. She couldn't stand that she was raising her children in such a bad environment.

With everything splintering in her life, Janet doubted so much about herself. She didn't think that she could be the mom her three children deserved, especially now that she was on her own to raise her kids. Her ex showed little interest in continuing his role as a father; though, he did help support her financially, which Janet had mixed feelings about. She knew her ex was toxic and abusive, so it was best that he stayed away from the kids, but she hated that the kids felt the absence of their father. They were hurting, and Janet blamed herself for their pain. Her oldest especially took the divorce hard, and Janet worried that his psyche would deeply be impacted by his family situation. She knew that something needed to change or she would never be happy regardless of the blessing in her life. It was hard for her to even imagine change. Her life had been filled with self-doubt for so long.

Fortunately, Janet recognized the need to change, so she looked for help. It was a gradual change, and she was reluctant at first, but she was committed to the process. She took measures to detach herself from her ex-husband. After a short stay with her sister, she moved her kids to a new house so the family could have a fresh start. She made a concerted effort to get a promotion at work (which she didn't get for several years), and she strived to figure out who she was beyond who her husband told her who she was.

She also knew that she had to specifically address her self-esteem. She started talking to a therapist and took to the library for some self-help books. I asked her once what made her decide to change, and she told me, "When I saw my daughter, I started thinking about how if I didn't make a change, she could end up just like me. Insecure and struggling for decades. I didn't want that for her, and I didn't want that for me either." Janet needed to do better for the sake of her family, and she was determined to fight her demons so that her children wouldn't have to grow up as she did. She wanted them to be confident and secure in themselves.

Today, years later, Janet is a confident woman. She talks with a spirited tone, and her shoulders are held high. Her smile is self-assured, and she talked spiritedly about her family. Everything about her has changed. She's put the effort in to build up the self-esteem that she lost in childhood and during the time she spent with her abusive husband. She learned a lot about herself in the process, and she was able to find new passions that she could feel good about.

She's content with her position at her job. She enjoys time with her kids without worrying that she's an awful mother. She can eat food without feeling the need to purge it. She's forgiven her parents for the harm that they did her in the past. She still has moments when she reverts to having low self-esteem when she is triggered by certain life events or circumstances, but, for the most part, she has freed herself of her self-doubt, and she has learned to believe in herself and her skills. When I first talked to her, I was in awe of her journey. I admired the way she took charge of her life and decided that she had enough of being insecure. While it's never easy to make changes, ultimately, anyone can do what Janet did and gain confidence.

CHAPTER 2
Common Insecurities

Insecurities feed into self-confidence issues. Thus, it helps to know what common insecurities people have so that you can combat the things that make you insecure and grow your self-esteem. The more insecurities that linger, the harder it will be to build your self-esteem. You need to begin fighting your insecurities and learning about what makes you feel most insecure. It takes time to understand the roots of your low self-esteem, but when you put in that effort, you'll realize how necessary it is to your well-being. The sooner you start, the sooner you will feel better. You can even start analyzing your insecurities as you read through this chapter!

Past Experiences

Past experiences inevitably lead to future ones, and they define your present if you let them. The wounds that were left in your past become scars, and that's how it is supposed to be. They are part of you, but for some people, those wounds never become scars. They fester, and they remain fresh on your skin as scabbed over wounds that you keep picking open. You don't give them the time or the attention that they need to heal. You try to ignore them away, hoping that they will vanish on their own, but that's never the case. If only it was!

Past failures are one of the biggest experiences that influences present behaviors. Failure can make you feel like you are not worth anything, and when you fail, sometimes instead of taking it in stride and using it to improve your life, you attribute it to something being wrong with you. You think that your failure means that you are incompetent, stupid, or lack something else when that's not the case. The most successful people have had past failures. They use those failures to grow and do better. Failures don't have to be related to your worth. They can be used to motivate you to grow as a person.

Trauma can come in many forms, and they are always bad. It can be through either physical or emotional trauma. While physical trauma can be hard, it's often the emotional aspects of trauma that hurt people the most. Emotional trauma can come in the form of abuse, mental health issues, bullying, grief, and anything else that causes you emotional trauma. Any of these things can linger and develop into something more if they are untreated. Never belittle your trauma. Whatever trauma you have, it's important even if it feels insignificant. Just because someone has it worse doesn't mean your trauma doesn't impact you!

Abuse is one of the most significant traumas that a person can face, and it is also one of the largest influencers in self-esteem because abuse often uses manipulation techniques that warp people's mindsets. When people experience abuse, they try to rationalize what is happening to them, and often, the logic they use is twisted. They start to blame themselves for their own suffering. They become ashamed of themselves based on what happened to them. Not all abuse victims react the same, but many follow the same patterns, and it is common for abuse to impact abuse survivors' mentalities.

Even positive things that have happened in your past can be turned into negatives when you have low self-esteem. You can become convinced that good things that happen to you have nothing to do with your skills while when bad things happen to you they have everything to do with your lack of skills. People may undermine those past successes and find a way to mark them as somehow inadequate. I've heard from people, like Janet, who have graduated second in their class but still were hung up on the fact that they couldn't be number one. If you find yourself shrugging off your accomplishments or excusing them away, you may be turning your positives into negatives.

Whatever has happened in your past, it doesn't have to be your future. You are not defined by your past choice or by whatever has happened to you. You do get to decide what you do going forward, and look at that as a chance to build your self-esteem. Your self-esteem thrives when you take control of your life, and by controlling what your past means to you you can feel better about yourself.

The Unknown

Another major influencer is the fear of the unknown. Life comes with so many unknowns that can leave you unable to keep up with all the changes that you've been making. You can become overwhelmed with all the thoughts of what might happen. People you love may die. You may lose a beloved pet. Maybe you'll get in a car accident. You don't know what tomorrow will bring, and that can make you doubt your future. When you don't know what might happen, it's easy to let doubt creep in. The unknown is not something that we can change, but it something that you can make peace with.

Career

A person's career is one of the most profound areas of their life. Thus, it can be a cause of common insecurity that leads to low self-esteem. You spend much of your time in your career, and society considers it one of the most important areas in a person's life. People are judged by our society based on their career success. For years, people work to build their careers, and the idea that they might not experience the success that they want in their careers can be devastating. If you feel you are not where you should be with your career, you may start to feel insecure.

Your job title may be one part of your job that is causing you to doubt yourself, and your payment is another that may make you doubt your worth to your company. Titles and payment are often seen as markers of how good you are at your job. They give you seniority and authority over other employees competing in the same field, but they do not express your worth. While it is easy to get so caught up in your career that you feel it is your entire worth, it is not healthy to think that way, nor does it get you any farther in life.

People often commonly doubt their work product as well. They think that they can never do their work well enough to get the accolades and success that they crave. Projects become nightmarish as they worry about never living up to the expectations that are held for those projects. The worry about letting their bosses and/ or employees down. It doesn't help anyone to worry about not doing good enough work rather than fully using your brainpower to do the best work you can. Worrying takes up mental space that you cannot afford to lose.

Whatever it is that bothers you at work; you need to address it as soon as you can. You spend so much time at work, and if you let bad feelings linger, you are bound to hate your job. Further, negative thoughts towards your job also mean that you will not do your work thoroughly as you might if you felt good about your position at work. Psychologically, you will back away and disengage from what you are doing, which never ends well in a professional setting. Don't become a self-fulfilling prophecy, and let your doubts come true. Doubts do come true if you don't fight them, so fight them!

Body Image

Looks are one of the main areas that cause people to worry. Society often judges people based on how they look. These expectations aren't always fair because of the unrealistic standards that have been created by the beauty industry and the wellness industry. People are harsh on their bodies based on standards that most normal people will never achieve. It's too easy to look at the model and wish to look like she does without realizing that the model has likely been photoshopped, and she might not be healthy. The media deceives us into thinking that we should look different when we are probably fine just as we are.

Societal expectations can be deadly. Eating disorders are some of the most deadly mental health disorders, and they are fuelled by low self-esteem. Often, these disorders start in adolescence, and they can continue through adulthood. These conditions are hard to treat, and some people never recover from them. While the causes of these disorders are complex, one major cause is the emphasis on how bodies should look. Young people do not see a wide range of healthy bodies, and they are not taught to value what their bodies can do rather than what their bodies look like. People need to learn that what society expects of bodies is different than what is good for bodies.

Many people see themselves in different ways than other people see them. Women especially tend to hate their bodies, which leads to deep self-hate. People look in the mirror, and they can immediately find something that they think is wrong with them. They'll say that they have too much fat or their nose is too big, but often, these criticisms have no direct relationship to their health. People are tearing themselves apart and compromising their self-esteem because society tells them that they are not acceptable as they are, and that false thought that people aren't enough or don't look the way they should is so harmful and crippling to people suffering from their self-image.

The dieting industry encourages your low self-esteem. As a seventy billion industry that continues to grow despite obesity rising (showing that it makes no real change), the dieting industry makes money by using your insecurities against you. They convince you that your body can be better than what it is, and they encourage unrealistic images that make you want to be another person entirely. You don't have to continue engaging with his hateful industry that tries to sell you products that don't work. Free yourself from the binds of wanting to change and accept yourself as you are.

Try to look at your body based on what it does rather than what it looks like. Your body can do incredible things, and what it can do has nothing to do with how it looks. You can be the least socially acceptable looking person and still excel in your pursuits. You don't need to give into beauty standards. Use beauty and wellness products that make you feel good rather than ones that make you feel bad without ever doing anything to boost your self-esteem. You don't have to feel ugly anymore because your beauty is in all the actions you can do with your lovely body as it exists right now.

Health

Your health isn't something that you can control, which makes it a source of insecurity for many people. You may also feel responsible for the physical and emotional well-being of other people in your life. When a loved one becomes sick, you may have to take on a caretaking role. In this caretaking role, you may begin to have self-esteem issues. You may feel as though you cannot take care of the person you love well-enough, which makes you doubt your abilities and worth as a person. If someone you love dies, you may wonder if there was something else you could've done to prolong your life despite doing as much as you could have. Of course, these thoughts are often not rational, but they are common. It's easy to blame yourself for hard circumstances, even when there is no rhyme or reason to them. The health of yourself and the health of your loved ones impact your thoughts about yourself.

Brain

Just as you can doubt your body or your health, you can doubt your brainpower. You can think that you are not good enough for academic pursuits, and you can feel insecure when you are around super-intelligent people who seem to know more than you. When you doubt your brain, you start to doubt your entire thought process. Everything you try becomes something you're "too stupid for." The truth is that your intelligence doesn't change who you are. You're the same wonderful person regardless of your IQ! Let go of the idea that you have to be Einstein to have a remarkable brain. All brains are remarkable. They're just remarkable in other ways.

People with lower intelligence are often looked down upon, which sends the wrong message to people who have unique skill sets that don't follow the traditional intelligence standards. They are treated like they are lesser beings even though they are merely different beings. If you have a lower IQ, people might look at you like you're a subpar human, or they might treat you like a child who doesn't understand anything. Even if your IQ isn't high, that doesn't mean you're dumb because there are more forms of intelligence than just IQ. Some people are better at knowing how to converse with others while some are better at technical skills. Whatever intelligence you have, there's no reason to feel ashamed of it.

Likewise, people with less education are often also looked down upon regardless of actual intelligence. Intelligence is like height; it is part of you, and it impacts your life, but it does not define what kind of person you are or can be. The same is true of education. Having an education doesn't make you smarter or more talented. It only focuses on showing you how to use knowledge and skills. It does not dictate your worth. It doesn't matter how smart you are if you don't use intelligence in good ways, then you are wasting it. When you use whatever intelligence you have to the fullest, that's when you should feel good about yourself because that shows that you are using your brain power as much as you can. It's people who waste their brain power who should feel embarrassed. As long as you are using your brain to the fullest, who cares if you have a master's? Who cares if you have a doctorate? There's nothing wrong with having an education, but there's nothing wrong with sticking to a technical school or a two-year degree or no degree at all! Your education depends on you, and as long as you feel content with it, that's all that matters. You can also teach yourself skills if you want to learn more!

Even highly intelligent people can worry that they aren't smart enough. Some of the brightest people I know have thought that they were stupid. They felt like they'd never know enough, and I get what they mean. People will never have all the information in the world, nor could our brains handle it. There will always be things we don't understand, and there will always be times when we are wrong. This idea can be discouraging. It is a hard blow to our self-esteem that we will always be ignorant. Though, it doesn't have to hurt so much if we can learn to accept what we don't know. There's nothing wrong with not knowing! The whole point of life is to find out, to know things that we didn't know before.

Your brain is a gift, no matter what your intelligence or education levels. Your brain can do so many things, and it does so many things without you even having to think about it. It keeps you alive automatically, and that's pretty remarkable. You are remarkable, and you have so much potential to grow and learn throughout your life. You have skills and aptitudes that other people don't have. Embrace what your brain can do and build your skills rather than begrudging your brain for what it can't do. It's okay that you don't know everything. The smartest people know that there's so much greatness that lies within the unknown.

Wealth

How much money you have is something that is often linked to self-esteem. People think that their bank wallet says how well they are doing in life, but your bank balance can't tell you if you're a good person. It can't tell you if you are happy. It can't tell you to feel good about yourself. Your bank balance is just another piece of data that helps you navigate through life. It isn't you. You are not your money, and when you forget this fact, you lose your ability to feel self-assured when you don't have a whole lot of money. If I were to put Martin Luther King Jr. next to a billionaire, you wouldn't say that MLK Jr. is worse off simply because he had a smaller bank account. You don't judge the worth of others based on the money they have, so you shouldn't judge yourself that way either.

Money is one of the predominant concerns that people have in life. It's no wonder that this concern is so prominent because money allows people to put food on the table and to have shelter. It keeps them alive, so, naturally, people would want it. We all want money because we all need it to survive. One of the most common insecurities that men have is that they are not a good enough provider for their families. They hate the thought that their families will suffer because they don't make enough money, but money does not directly correlate to your worth. You are not worth more just because your bank account is. Stop thinking that you are worthless just because you don't have as much money as you'd like. Getting that money won't erase your self-esteem issues.

Making less money than others does not mean your job or that you are less important. Your salary does not define the validity of your job. Some jobs that aren't paid well are incredibly important. Sports stars get millions of dollars while teachers get barely enough to make ends meet. This is not to say that there's anything wrong with being a sports star, but the education of students, by most measures, is more important than entertainment. Thus, no career or salary should be belittled. People who are working are doing important roles in our society, so they deserve respect, and you deserve to respect your own contribution.

Your monetary success does not change who you are as a person. It doesn't matter how much money you make, your genes have not changed. You are the same person that you've always been. Money may make you act differently than you normally would, or the lack of money might also make you act differently, but they do not inherently change your core. Your personality isn't suddenly replaced. You don't become happier and healthier in the blink of an eye. IF I were to put a million dollars in your bank account right now, that money would make you happy, but seeing that number wouldn't change you in a flash. Money's not a cure-all solution.

You are more than your wealth, so stop acting as though success equals money. So many notable people died poor. So many artists didn't see a dime when they were alive. Don't get caught up in all the money that you don't have. Riches won't change much of anything self-esteem wise. It doesn't matter how much you make. If you are insecure, you are going to be insecure whether you have money or not. It's a hard pill to swallow, but the riches you dream of may solve some problems, but they won't cure your self-esteem; you'll just find other insecurities to focus on.

Social

Your social relationships are another huge factor that can cause you to feel insecure about yourself. Relationships or the lack of relationships can make you feel like you have little worth. Some people become too worried about who they know instead of getting to know the people in their lives. You are so much more than the people you know. The people you know are important because they are an important factor in your happiness, but you are not worth more if you have one hundred friends versus ten. Similarly, if you are dating someone - divorced married or single - it also doesn't influence your worth. It's okay to be alone if it makes you happy.

Romantic relationships are the most prominent area of insecurity for people. Many people fear that when they are not in a relationship, they are worth less than they would be in a relationship. They use relationships to validate themselves and would prefer having a toxic relationship to none at all. The need to always be with someone speaks to a deep self-esteem issue because you shouldn't need to always be dating someone to feel like you are valued. You should feel valued beyond just romantic relationships. Find ways to love yourself that don't require someone else loving you.

Parental relationships are another big factor in people's self-esteem. Our parents influence us from the day that we are born, sometimes for the better and sometimes for the worse. You have to be able to separate yourself from your parents and have your own identity. When you try too much to please your parents, you may lose track of yourself, which makes you feel identity-less. When you feel that you have no identity, your self-esteem plummets, so you need to forge an identity of your own to be healthy. You are your own person, and it's time to escape your familial shadow and embrace that person.

Just as your relationships with your parents matter, if you have kids, your relationships with your kids matter as well. Often, the relationship you had with your parents is reflected in your kids whether because you tried to avoid being like your parents or mimicked your parents. Having children is one of the most rewarding pursuits a person can accomplish, but it also comes with challenges that may make you fear inferior. You may doubt that you are doing what is best for your children, and you may feel certain that you are harming them inadvertently. Feeling like a bad parent can make it hard to keep a good balance between discipline and care, and it can blur boundaries that confuse the child. You need to be confident in your parenting skills to parent consistently and fairly.

Your friendships are some of the most important relationships that you have, and they can make you feel at your most confident, but sometimes, they can make you feel insecure too. Friends can make you feel better about yourself than anyone else, but they can also be toxic just as any relationship can. Some friends are overly critical and may take advantage of your insecurities. These friends are not real friends and are only using you. Focus on genuine friends who want you to be happy and attempt to make you feel better about yourself rather than worse. Positive friendships go a long way in helping you feel like you belong and establishing good self-esteem.

The relationships you have are vital to how you behave and how you feel about yourself. If your relationships are rocky and unstable, it will be hard to feel good about yourself, but if your relationships are strong and created with your own self-esteem in mind, they will help you maintain your self-esteem. All relationships that you have should make you feel good about yourself. People who insult you constantly and dismiss your worth are ones who you want to keep as far away from you as you can. They will only ever hurt you, and they don't have your best interests in mind.

CHAPTER 3
The Psychology Of Self-Esteem

Theories on Self-Esteem

Self-esteem is something that people have grappled with for hundreds of years, but the term itself is fairly young. The term was only introduced to psychology a mere one hundred and thirty years ago when the psychologist William James created his theory of self-esteem. In 1890, when James showed his theory to the world, the concept was still unstudied, and we have come a long way in understanding what self-esteem means and how it impacts people's lives. Even with all the work that has been done in the years since James' work, people still have a lot of research to do to better understand the psychological and neurological factors related to self-esteem.

William James' theory of self-esteem was rudimentary, but it opened the door to additional study about self-esteem, and it is still acknowledged as important even now. James said that self-esteem could be determined by a basic formula that was: success divided by "pretensions." Pretensions referred to the combination of what we believe we can achieve, our values, and our goals. Thus, to put this more understandably, when you achieve something that goes beyond what you imagined, you feel much better about yourself. Meanwhile, when you do worse than you hoped in your pursuit, you feel bad about yourself.

Thinkers Cooley and Mead continued research about self-esteem into the twentieth century using theories that focused on symbolic interactionism. Symbolic interactionism suggests that people's self-esteem correlates with the interactions that they have. Thus, while James suggested a rigid, universal view of why people have or don't have self-esteem, Cooley and Mead determined that self-esteem was more related to individual experiences and that self-esteem is created via our interactions with others and the world around us. Thus, our self-esteem profiles are unique, and we may have self-worth in some areas but not others. Cooley and Mead still suggested that society as a whole shaped what we consider success and therefore our self-worth, but we all interpret those expectations differently as we apply them to ourselves.

Later in the twentieth century, Stanley Coopersmith added some ideas of his own to self-esteem research. He furthered some of the ideas created by Cooley and Mead, but he added that self-esteem is often related to experiences during early childhood when people's expectations, personalities, and values are being formed. He suggested that children who felt loved and safe would have better self-esteem than those who did not have that good environment. He said that as people went through life that they would either add to the baseline created in childhood or subtract from it. Different experiences in adulthood would determine someone's self-esteem, which could change slightly throughout their life. While Coppersmith had some useful ideas, like all theorists, his theories alone did not show the full breadth of what self-esteem means.

Another twentieth-century theorist who worked around the same time as Coppersmith determined that self-esteem may be influenced more greatly by later childhood experiences. Morris Rodenberg determined that the tumultuous development during adolescence resulted in a person's self-esteem. As children go from children to adults, they begin to compare themselves more with others, and they begin to think that everything is related to them. For example, a child may see two girls laughing and then think those girls are laughing at them, even if that is not the case. They become more aware of their place in the world and start to ask themselves if they are meeting societal standards.

Beyond the early theorist who created ideas that build what researchers today label self-esteem, three predominant theories are still commonly found in self-esteem research. These theories all have different ways in which they are strong, and one may appeal to you more than others. It is unclear which theory is true, but by understanding the different outlooks on self-esteem, you can better understand how your self-esteem has been created in your own life.

The first theory of self-esteem is the Self-Determination Theory (SDT). This theory says that people who have high self-esteem have been able to thrive in their environments and explore them without being deprived of their basic needs, including psychological ones. It states that socially people are given the opportunities that they need to fulfill their needs and grow as people. This theory combines autonomy, relatedness, and competence. Autonomy is the idea that you can decide your own actions. Relatedness is the idea that you need certain social experiences that make you feel as though you fit into your society. Finally, competence is the idea that you need to be able to master certain tasks and skills. When you have all three of these, you have strong self-esteem, but when these components are missing, your self-esteem may suffer. Under this theory, self-esteem is firm and static. While self-esteem could change, it would take major factors to break it once you have it. Real self-esteem, more than just fleeting feelings of self-esteem, requires overall security in yourself that cannot be broken with a few doubts or minor psychological blows.

A second theory that researchers have used for self-esteem is Terror Management Theory (TMT). This theory posits that self-esteem is rooted in societal constructs, which means that things that society values become a huge part of how individuals see the world. This theory says that societies and large groups of people act according to what will make them feel less terror. Death is one of the biggest things that people are afraid of, so to respond to that fear, people have ideas in place that make them feel less afraid of death, which is an inevitable part of human life.

Thus, societies or groups of people act in ways that often further the idea of people "living on", even when they are dead. Accordingly, high-self esteem is related to one's ability to fit into the societal norms and to avoid that anxiety related to death. In this model, factors like believing in an afterlife can impact a person's anxiety about life and therefore influence their self-esteem. Thus, in this theory, self-esteem is widely social more than a person's success or the fulfillment of needs. TMT, because it relies on the single need to reduce the anxiety surrounding death, is not as resilient as the self-esteem depicted in the first theory. It is more likely to change, and it is reliant on cultural factors.

Some people want to combine the idea of TMT with attachment theory. Attachment theory is the idea that children attach to parents in ways that will increase their odds of survival, which leads to different attachment styles. Some children will have secure attachments, for example, and this attachment style is what makes kids feel the safest. Kids with this attachment style will feel well cared for, and while they do not enjoy seeing their caretaker leave, they will not have feelings of abandonment. Further, they will be glad when their parents return. These kids tend to have higher self-esteem than those with insecure attachment styles. Some theorists have suggested that attachment style is connected to how children look at the world. Just like TMT says that self-esteem is connected to the terror people feel about the world, attachment theory is related to the anxiety children feel about their attachments to their parents. Thus, these two theories can be combined, and children's attachment styles could be related to their views of society and their levels of terror about those societies.

The final theory is the Sociometer Theory (ST). This theory suggests that people require some level of belonging to thrive and to have self-esteem. Having people to relate to and a group to be a part of makes people feel meaning and gives social value to people's lives, which is a sociometer. Without this social value, it is hard for people to have a sense of worth or fulfillment. Further, this theory suggests that while it is positive to have integration into groups, people are more impacted by being left out of groups that they wish to belong to. When a person feels as though they cannot belong, they will feel less worth, and their self-esteem will, therefore, be lowered. Feeling belonging can then increase one's self-esteem. ST suggests that mood is one of the biggest indicators of self-esteem. People who are more anxious and shameful have lower self-esteem while those who feel at ease and proud have higher self-esteem. This theory, like TMT, is a single need theory that emphasizes the need to be part of something bigger than yourself. This theory suggests that self-esteem is more dynamic than the self-esteem depicted under SDT because it can change based on one need being unfulfilled. While some researchers still argue this theory, many think it is too simplistic of a view for self-esteem.

While there are many different theories for self-esteem, the history of self-esteem research and the three theories listed are some of the most common ideas that still circulate in psychological circles. Some researchers have suggested that true self-esteem is a combination of bits and pieces from various theories. Self-esteem likely is created by both social factors and human needs, both physical and psychological. Thus, it is crucial to consider both when contemplating self-esteem.

Self-Esteem Research

Self-esteem research has been questioning the relationship between certain facets of human life and self-esteem. These studies have often shown profound links between societal issues and self-esteem. Further, they have shown how vital it is to improve your self-esteem so that you can grow and thrive as a person. While there are people with low self-esteem who do well in life, the research shows that people with high self-esteem are happier and healthier. The more you can develop your self-esteem, the better you will feel, and looking at the research, you can better see what influences self-esteem.

Studying the correlation between self-esteem and success is one of the most prominent self-esteem research. Studies have found that of girls who are fifteen to seventeen, seventy percent have avoided doing certain activities when they don't like the way they look. Some studies show that there is little correlation between success and self-esteem; however, there are factors related to high self-esteem that indirectly link to success. While people with self-esteem can be successful, they may limit how much they do. For example, they may not take a promotion or they may not even apply to their dream job because they do not think that they are good enough for it. Thus, people with low self-esteem will put their best efforts into what they are doing (and sometimes overcompensate), but they may not try to strive to do more than what they are currently doing. Thus, they will miss out on important opportunities for success. Further, people with low self-esteem are less likely to feel successful regardless of their actual success.

Self-esteem and depression and anxiety as well as other mental health issues have been studied extensively. People who have low self-esteem are more likely to be mentally ill, and self-esteem has long been linked to conditions like depression and anxiety. Research has suggested that happiness is the most influential factor of self-esteem. There is a forty-seven percent link between happiness and self-esteem. People who have low self-esteem are not only more likely to be mentally ill, but they are also less able to cope with the symptoms of their mental illness when they have self-esteem. Thus, low self-esteem exacerbates existing problems. People with self-esteem struggle to live normally. Three-fourths of teenage girls who had low self-esteem used harmful coping mechanisms such as self-harm, substance abuse, disordered eating, smoking, or harmful behaviors to others to deal with their feelings of inadequacy.

Another important area of study that researchers have delved into is self-esteem and race. People of marginalized races are more likely to have social issues that influence their self-esteem. Studies have shown that in the United States, black people have the highest rate of self-esteem issues among any of the races. Increased rates of discipline in school and incarceration as they grow up, racial minorities struggle to understand how they fit into the larger society. Further, stereotypes such as black people, particularly black girls, being more aggressive and more sexually active, feeds into a society that inherently demeans the worth of those who are not white. These stereotypes result in other issues such as sexual assault, body image issues, and countless other systemic issues that can be seen in any part of ordinary life. Young black people are made to feel lesser, which correlates to lower levels of self-esteem. Thus, black youth show up to school less and are unable to get the foundation they need. While many black youths work hard to go to school and get an education, even their needs often aren't met, and their history is whitewashed. Non-white kids are marked as "other," and this otherness makes it hard for them to fit into their society and feel reassured about who they are.

Other groups of people who are marginalized can also suffer from increased rats of low self-esteem. Just like race matters, the way people's bodies look matter as well. Weight stigma is one of the most common lookist stigmas in Western society. The judgment of fat people as lazy and undisciplined is fatphobic and erroneous. Unfortunately, those stereotypes make it hard for fat people, or those without idealized bodies, to fit into society. Fat people are often mocked and abused by fatphobic people, making them feel worse about themselves (which can lead to weight gain). Research has shown that it is more unhealthy to be five pounds underweight than seventy pounds overweight; yet, the five pounds underweight is often glorified while the overweight person is mocked. People who are overweight go through life feeling like they are lesser, even if they are otherwise healthy and happy.

Similarly, people who are not of the dominant religion of their culture can be made to feel like outsiders. Muslims in America, for example, may be called terrorists or looked upon with skepticism despite being ordinary people. Alternatively, Jews still face antisemitism across the world, and this can be seen easily in stereotypes such as Jewish people being greedy. Again, these pervasive ideas are false, but they exist and harm the self-esteem of those who are the subjects of those stereotypes. The negative views society has of those who are different ensures that people who are not in power are hurt by a lack of self-esteem.

Women and people who embrace feminine things are often outcast as well. While women are not in a minority, they are marginalized. Women have increased rates of illnesses such as eating disorders, and an unfair emphasis is often put on their bodies. Women are praised for what they look like rather than what they can do, which is why life can be so confusing for young girls who are enduring bodily changes and worrying about their weight, sexual assault and harassment, and everything else kids face. Women have been made to feel lesser than men for so long that even when they are just as qualified, women feel that they cannot compete. Studies have found that in the political sphere, women are less likely to run for office unless they feel that they are completely qualified whereas men will run even if they don't have all the qualifications. Thus, women feel less assured about their abilities to complete tasks and do a good job even if they are more qualified than their male counterparts.

People who are in the LGBT+ community also experience bigotry that can result in lowered self-esteem. They are more likely to harm themselves or commit suicide, and they have higher rates of eating disorders, anxiety, and depression. These mental dysfunctions have some correlation to low self-esteem. Being marked as outsiders and even hated by other people, it can be hard to have a sense of belonging and to have emotional needs fulfilled. Some LGBT youth are rejected by their families and do not even have access to their basic physical needs. Thus, the LGBT community often suffers from low self-esteem.

All groups, especially the marginalized, must be considered when looking at self-esteem. Self-esteem impacts much of human behavior. Thus, early self-esteem issues can lead to lifelong ones, which is why it's so important to remember the role of things like race, body religion, gender, and sexuality on self-esteem. The research continues to show how various groups and self-esteem are interrelated. Further, it delves into how self-esteem impacts people's lives. Researchers have learned a lot about self-esteem in one hundred and thirty years. Though, there is still plenty for researchers to learn. Hopefully, researchers will continue to pay attention to this important topic so that we have an even better understanding of self-esteem and its role in our lives.

CHAPTER 4
Face Your Trauma'

Trauma is something that every person experiences. No matter who you are or happy your life is as a whole, trauma is unavoidable. Bad things happen to good people, and you can't prevent them from happening. Nevertheless, your trauma doesn't have to destroy your self-esteem, you can face your trauma and show yourself that no matter how bad you felt in the past that you want to feel good going into the future. Trauma will never stop hurting you. It will always come back in pangs, but it doesn't have to control your future if you step up and face all those hurts you don't want to face.

Become More Aware of Your Past Self

Your past self is someone you can't escape. It doesn't matter who you are now, that person you were in the past is very much alive through memory (and probably some old pictures). Even if you did bad things in the past, you don't have to hate yourself now. It's easy to get caught up in the past if you don't make room for that past in your present. You try to eliminate all memories of who you were, but you need to stop trying to forget and remember what you didn't like about the past and why you never want to go back. Remind yourself how your future can be better and how you can use that trauma to learn and grow. No matter the painful experience, you can grow from it. That doesn't mean you wouldn't want to change it if you could go back in time. What it means is that it happened, you can't go back in time, and you're committed to moving on from your bad experience.

Let yourself remember what you've experienced in the past, and think about how you used to feel in the past. Let all the bad memories hit you. Cry if you need to, but don't avoid those memories. Also, remember the good ones. Maybe your dad was abusive, but if you have a good memory, don't feel like you need to erase it because of all the bad he did. Just because someone hurt you doesn't mean you have to invalidate all the good memories. Those memories can exist while still remembering all the trauma that someone caused. Also, remember a time when you felt free from all the pain. Think of when you felt good, and hold onto that feeling. It's not always easy to acknowledge who you used to be, but it is necessary.

Accept What Has Happened to You

What has happened to you is something that you need to accept. You don't need to like it but accept the trauma. Admit the wrongs that have been done to you, and know that what other people did to you was not your fault. Also admit the wrongs you've done to others because by admitting those wrongs, you can begin to forgive yourself for your mistakes. Don't deny or repress all the traumas of the past. Honor them for being a part of your life because they were even if they weren't a good part.

Forgive the people who wronged you. This is a hard thing to do. When people hurt you, sometimes you want to hold a grudge. You don't have to restore relationships with people who hurt you, but staying angry at them only eats at your self-esteem. It makes it almost impossible for you to move on. Forgiveness is something that you do for yourself because it marks that the person who hurt you no longer has power over you or how you identify yourself. You are a free person able to love yourself in ways that other people failed to do.

It helps you mend the wounds of the past when you accept the trauma that you cannot change. It can be hard to think about past traumas that have influenced you, but they are vital parts of your self-esteem, so you can't avoid addressing those traumas forever. Trauma only gets harder to manage the longer you put it on the back burner, so it's time to bring your trauma into the light. Shine the light into your trauma's eyes and see that it is not you. You are more than the things or the people that hurt you.

Get Help If You Need It

Sometimes, you cannot deal with your trauma alone. It probably isn't even wise to deal with your traumas alone. Humans are social creatures, so it can be advantageous to add social interactions to your self-development process. The more you can be open with other people, the easier it will be to free yourself of the self-doubt and shame that may be associated with your low self-esteem.

Talk to a friend or a family member. When you open up to someone you love, that is an important step in getting better and addressing the trauma that has so wounded you. The more you can open up, the less secretive your trauma will feel, and the shame will melt away. Being open is difficult, and it's one of the hardest things that a person can do, but it is well worth the payout because not only does it help you improve your self-esteem, but it also allows you to make deeper connections with the people in your life who are most important to you. Sharing about yourself is one of the best ways to build relationships, and those relationships will help you feel more confident and secure. Of course, don't feel like you have to tell something to anyone you don't trust, but if you do trust someone, it can be great to get some pent up feelings off your chest.

Go to a therapist. Therapy is a great option for people who need help but don't feel comfortable turning to a loved one or who need more help than a loved one can provide. There's nothing shameful about needing help from a professional. For those who can afford it, anyone can benefit from therapy because it gives people a safe place to talk. Even therapists have therapists, so therapy isn't something that has to be reserved for mentally ill people. Anyone who needs a little help in finding and appreciating themselves can benefit too. If it's an option that's available to you, there's no reason you shouldn't try it.

If you need help, don't be afraid to ask for it. People who know when to ask for help are more confident. They know that needing help doesn't take away from their autonomy or value as an individual. Knowing when to get help is a sign of emotional maturity, and it ensures that you suffer in silence. When you put a name to your self-esteem issues, and you don't let them be secret anymore, you cannot be embarrassed by them. You take away the power they have over you, and you fight them with the little spark of confidence that everyone always has somewhere deep inside of them.

Julius: A Case Study

Julius began his life modestly in a third-floor walk-up in Chicago. He was a middle child, so he'd never been alone in his life. Both his parents had big families who were major parts of their lives, so Julius was never alone. He always had people to keep him entertained. Though, his parents weren't around all the time. His parents worked hard to bring in enough money to support themselves, Julius, and his four siblings, but they always had food on the table. They laughed a lot, and they loved to watch movies together, so Julius always said that his family was a chaotic, loving environment. It was busy, but he loved them.

Their two-bedroom apartment was packed, especially when Julius' grandma got sick and had to move in with the family just before she died or when they had family get-togethers. When his grandmother died, it was hard on the family. They had more space, but the chair where she used to sit felt empty, and to Julius, it was hard dealing with his house being a little quieter. He wishes he had longer with her. He was only eight when she died.

The family lived a hard-life, but they loved each other, and they did their best to support each other even if his parents didn't have a lot of time for recreation. Every so often, they'd go to weekend trips to camp, and Julius remembered those days fondly. He loved his family, and while troublesome at times, his family was a comfort for him.

His life was happy enough, but Julius had problems when he started going to school. He liked school at first, but after a while, it became clear that he wasn't like the other kids. He made a few friends, but it was hard for him to relate to the other kids. He had undiagnosed dyslexia at the time, which made school hard for him to do well at school. Kids made fun of him for being stupid, and the bullying got worse when he entered junior high. It continued through high school. Julius was diagnosed with dyslexia by then, and his parents didn't understand it, but they supported him as best as they could, and Julius taught himself how to manage his condition. He ended up proving that he wasn't dumb. He made pretty good grades. He didn't fail a single class in high school or even get a D, but his peers still called him dumb and useless, among other cruel words. Julius had always been adventurous. He'd loved trying wild tricks on his skateboard, and he dreamed of doing other extreme activities like skydiving. He was smart, and he wanted to someday do something that made a profound difference. He loved trying new things and expanding his skills, but the more he put up with bullying, the harder it was for him to try new things. He became "locked up" within himself, and he withdrew from his friend circle, choosing to spend most of his time alone. His family became concerned when Julian started acting differently. He was a quieter version of himself. He looked sad all the time, and the adventurous spirit was missing. Julius couldn't wait to get out of school and start a life away from the bullies. He imagined how great his life would be. He thought that when he was out of school he could finally feel confident, but things didn't work out as he expected.

When he was done with school, Julius got a decent job working at a law firm. He would have liked to be a lawyer, but higher education wasn't in the cards for him, so he did his best with what he had, and he worked long hours at the firm, trying to earn a living. He was good at his job, but he worried that he was dumb. Every time he made a mistake, he would feel an animalistic fear arise, and he'd be sure that he was going to get fired. His boss applauded his efforts, but couldn't hear any of the compliments between the constructive criticism. Constructive criticism felt like the end of the world. Each day he went into work, Julius would worry about what might happen. He'd worry so much sometimes that it would make him sick. He tried to ignore the constant dread in his stomach, but it didn't seem to want to go away.

When Julius got married to his wife, Sandra, and had a little boy with her, he began to worry about his role as a provider even more, which his father had always worried about as well. He would stay up late at night fretting over his ability to earn money to support his family. They had a small house, and they lived a nice life with picnics with family and holidays spent in the sunny living room. Julius' son, Alfie, was growing fast, and Julius and Sandra were considering expanding their little family. It didn't matter how great his life seemed, Julius still worried. With everything going so well, it felt like bad things were bound to happen. The clock was ticking, and Julius wasted so much energy imagining when that time would be. The self-doubt made it hard for Julius to ever feel secure. He was funny and adored by everyone, but he hated himself. He wanted to feel happy, but he didn't know how to improve his awful relationship with himself.

His doubts were only increased when Julius was let go from his job. This was the very thing that his low self-esteem had told him would happen. The problem hadn't been that he'd been a bad employee. He had been one of the best at the firm, working harder than even some of the lawyers, but the firm was having money problems, so they'd had to make adjustments, and Julius' role had been marked as unnecessary. After ten years on the job, Julius was thrust back into the scary job market. As he searched for a job, things got tense between him and his wife. They were fighting more because of money. Expenses were adding up, and Julius knew that he needed to get back on his feet if he ever wanted to feel better. He never felt so useless as the time when he was unemployed, but he was determined to prove his doubts wrong and be a good provider.

Eventually, Julius found another law firm he liked and got a job there. The job excited him in theory, but when he arrived for his first day, he got dismayed. His new job was at a legal clinic that focused on immigration law. Being a child of immigrants himself, Julius liked the cause that the firm was supporting, so when a rare support staff role popped up, he grabbed it. Unfortunately, the job was long hours without paying a lot. He ran himself weary, and then he'd drag his feet home, and he would be too tired to run around with his son in the backyard. He worried he wasn't being a good enough father, and while things had settled between him and his wife, money was still tight, and it still took a lot of budgeting to make sure they had enough money for everything.

Julius felt awful for not making enough money. His wife was a nurse, so she made a sufficient, though underpaid, second income, but they were far from wealthy, and with a son who they wanted to have any future he wanted, Julius drove himself crazy with all the feelings of insufficiency that he had. He looked at his kid and wanted to give him everything. What little sleep he was getting became unsatisfying. He started fighting with his wife more (yet again) and he was less patient with his son. He was taking his anger out on his family, and he didn't like that about himself. He felt like a monster, and he didn't know how to go back to being a happy husband and father. He was feeling depressed and didn't know his place in the world.

Julius did not like the person he had become, and that feeling deepened his self-hate. Julius knew that he needed to change because if he didn't, he would always be stuck in his cycle of feeling inadequate and then making everyone in his life feel worse about themselves because of his own self-worth issues. He didn't like who he was when he was insecure, so he knew that he had to change it. That revelation didn't come overnight, though. It was years before he finally made the tentative decision to change his course and take charge of his feelings about himself.

He knew that his problems stemmed from his childhood trauma of being bullied, which left him feeling insecure and worthless, so Julius addressed those traumas he experienced as a youngster to try to make sense of his past and release the grip that painful past had on him. Some of the trauma was harder to deal with than he expected. He did work to figure out who he was beyond his negative feelings about himself. It was painful to face some of the memories of what the other kids had done to him, but when he faced those feelings, they lost their control over him. He realized that he'd built them up in his head for no reason.

Julius is an example of how past pains can hurt you. Julius was no longer the kid who was being bullied, but he still felt that way for years after he finished school. He'd tried to ignore the negative feelings associated with bullying, but every so often they popped up again, and he would feel like a fresh wound was being poked. He felt silly for being so consumed by something so distant, but as he did some work to improve himself, he realized that his past was something that he couldn't ignore. He needed to acknowledge his pains and the insecurities the bullying left before he could heal.

Chapter 5
Learn Who You Are

Why You Need to Know Yourself

It isn't easy to discover who you are, but it is vital. Too many people lose track of themselves. They go through their lives pretending to be someone else, a person who can never make them happy. There are so many reasons that you need to learn who you are, and they all boil down to the idea that self-esteem requires an identity. If you feel like you have no identity, you aren't going to self-assure. You'll want to spend your life hiding away from who you are, which will only make you feel aimless and unfulfilled.

When you know yourself, you can feel good about yourself. How wonderful does it feel when you can have a conversation with someone and not feel like you have to hide certain parts with yourself? When you talk to your best friend, hopefully, you can feel free to speak your mind without judgment or being shamed. Shame is the feeling you get when you keep something hidden. If you have a lot of secrets, you are bound to feel shame. You will also confuse yourself. You'll pretend that you are someone different, unsure of who you really are.

Knowing yourself puts you closer to accepting and respecting yourself. If you take the time to get to know yourself, it is easier to curate self-love and compassion. If you don't know someone, you don't know how to properly respect them. You can treat them with basic human decency, but you can't treat them in a way that is more specific for them. The same is true of yourself. If you're in denial about who you are, you'll treat yourself in a way that is more fitting for the person you think that you are rather than the one who you really are. Denying yourself hurts you, and it makes you reject yourself every day rather than embracing yourself.

You can't be friends with someone who you don't know, so you can't like yourself if you're a stranger. If you don't know yourself, you're basically always interacting with a stranger. You're going into each situation treating yourself like someone you've just met. You can't move forward with that mindset. You end up spinning in circles, unsure about why your outcomes never change. Stop making yourself dizzy and instead get to know who you are. Stop being a stranger with yourself, and you'll find that so many opportunities will open up. You're worth knowing, and you should be excited about learning more about yourself.

You may not love the person you discover right away. The person who you really are may be someone you have learned to hate. That's common when people have low self-esteem, but it doesn't mean that you shouldn't work through those uncomfortable feelings. While it may be a little uncomfortable now, it is those feelings that will lead to self-discovery and personal growth. The more you can face your uncomfortable feelings, the less power they will have over you. You need to be able to look in the mirror and recognize the person you see. If you can't, you have more work to do.

Why You May Not Know Yourself

You need to know who you are, but you may not who you are because of years of denying yourself your personality. When you hate yourself, you inevitably learn to hate everything that you are. You try to dismiss those traits that you hate, and to find some sense of confidence; you try to convince yourself that those traits aren't a part of you. You lose track of who you are because of all the confusing messages that swirl around you and contradict one another. Fear not, you can find yourself again. It will take time and effort, but you can find yourself beneath all the chaos.

Some people repress themselves to the point that they don't know who they are. They tell themselves that they are not something so many times that they don't know who they are. Because of other issues, your brain may have denied you some of the key traits of your personality. Usually, repression happens when societal standards don't match up to who you are. You try to fit in, even when fitting in feels like an act of war against yourself. You think that the only well to do well in life is to pretend to be someone you're not. You get very good at fooling yourself, even though deep down you know that you are lying about who you are.

People can lose themselves in other things like their jobs. Sometimes, losing yourself goes beyond repression. Sometimes, your identity becomes so linked to one part of your life that you forget all the other areas of yourself. You're not trying to shut those parts down because you hate them, but you are favoring parts of yourself that may not be as fulfilling as the ones you are ignoring. It's common for people to be workaholics and forget all parts of themselves that don't have to do with work, but people are so much more than one hat they wear (parent, employee, boss, spouse, etc.). They are composites of all their roles, and that needs to be something that you take into account.

People can also lose themselves in other people. Some people have strong personalities, and that isn't necessarily a bad thing, but when people have strong personalities, it is easy to get lost in them. It is easy to be intoxicated by that person and to want to be just like them rather than being yourself. For people who already have low self-esteem, being someone else can feel like a welcome escape, but it is dangerous to get consumed by other people and let them define who you are. You aren't the same as them, and you cannot pretend to be.

It's easy to forget who you are, but it's also dangerous. When you lose track of yourself, you cannot feel confident. If you are repressing, hiding, or ignoring vital parts of yourself, you are not being genuine, and you are not acting in ways that will lead to happiness. You need to relinquish yourself from the parts of your life that make you feel not like yourself.

You need to embrace who you are no matter how hard that is sometimes. Being yourself can sometimes cause pain, but there's no other option if you want to feel confident. The bottom line is that you can be yourself, or you can be no one at all.

Challenge What People Say You Are

Because people's opinions often define how you see yourself (more on that later), it is often hard to establish identity. Knowing who you are should be something that comes so naturally, but with all the other ideas that we receive from others, it's not as simple as you would think. Finding who we are is sometimes a lifetime struggle, and for some people, it is a struggle that is never accomplished. People love lying to themselves, especially about themselves, and it is time that you stop lying because the more you lie to yourself and let others lie to you, the harder it will be to find your identity.

Find ways to look at yourself through your own lens. Stop using the perspectives of other people to color your view of yourself. We all have different eyes and vantage points. You need to see yourself through your own eyes and vantage points. You can use other people's perspectives to help you figure out yourself, but you cannot solely use those perspectives as an easy way of self-discovery. Letting yourself be mere what other people say you are is cheating, and it doesn't help you get anywhere. You end up being more confused than you ever were before!

Know that you can frame yourself however you want. If you want to be a certain person, you can shape yourself to look that way. You're in control of your narrative, so again, don't fall into the trap of lying to yourself. Frame yourself in a fair way that gives you confidence. You will never be able to look at yourself without bias, but you need to try to look at yourself as holistically as possible. There's nothing wrong with having flaws just as there's nothing wrong with having positive attributes. Those things are both parts of who you are. They have shaped you, so don't let your perception of yourself be too weighted by either perspective. Other people may see you as good or evil, but you can see the nuances within yourself.

You're in charge of what you say you are. You can identify however you want to regardless of what other people say about that identification. You can't control how people respond to the things you identify as, but if you want to identify a certain way, no one can stop you. You get to add the meaning to your personality. You define the meaning of your traits. You give life to them. It is hard to see all that makes you yourself because there is so much, but surely, there are certain parts of yourself that stand out.

Be honest, but also be merciful with how you identify yourself. Don't be judgmental. Hold yourself accountable, but don't tear yourself down for every little thing that you don't love. Being gentle with yourself is a great way to improve your self-esteem, and there's really no purpose in being too strict with yourself. Stop holding yourself to the unreal standards that other people put on you. Have your own standards, and cherish those standards. Your worth is self-defined, meaning that you get to set the parameters in any way that you want. Self-worth isn't defined by the standards of others. Your identity is completely up to you.

Evaluate What You Like

It's shocking how many people I've encountered who have completely forgotten what they like. I ask them about their hobbies, and they freeze as they try to think of what beyond their jobs or families gives them joy. They end up coming up with something half-hearted that I can immediately tell isn't their true passion. It's scary to think about how many people simply don't think about what they like. They haven't taken the time to evaluate their interests because they are so caught up in what they think that they're supposed to be. Those people may struggle to feel confident in themselves because their identities are floating around their heads, untethered.

Think back to yourself as a child. What did you like then? Your childhood interests can hint about what you like today. While interests do change, sometimes childhood interests fall out of favor because they are inconvenient rather than because you stopped liking them. My cousin liked to tap dance. She was pretty good at it too, but then she had a foot injury that made it hard to dance anymore. The injury has since healed, but it led to her quitting tap dance. Now that she's older, she'd like to start tap again, but she feels that she is too old. She's not too old. You're never too old for hobbies and interests, but society often discourages the continuation of certain activities. The goal isn't to be as good at them or as competitive at them as when you were a kid, but it can be fun to reinvent old hobbies. You'll never be a soccer star again, but kicking the ball around can still help you feel closer to yourself.

Determine if there are interests that you've pushed away that you'd like to have again. Just like the example of my cousin who wanted to try tap dancing again, think about things that you have quit. Find interests that you said you'd outgrown but really still yearn to indulge. Stop having guilty pleasures. You don't need to feel guilty for enjoyment. You can like things that seem frivolous or aren't going to help you further your life in any way. You need time when you can just relax without worrying about having to accomplish something.

Stop finding excuses to push away what you like. There's no reason to deprive yourself. You wouldn't want your loved ones to quit things that they loved only because they felt those things were somehow beneath them. The only time you should resist your wants is when they are harmful to yourself or others, but in most cases, the things that you deny yourself are things that you have no good reason to push away. Don't let anyone tell you that you can't like anything. If you like a trashy TV show, enjoy it! Who cares if it isn't intellectual? Who cares if it isn't something that you would normally like?

Your interests are important. Don't let anyone tell you that you shouldn't like a perfectly harmless hobby. If your hobby isn't hurting anyone else, there's no need not to do it. Don't let yourself feel shame over what you like. It's not juvenile to be passionate. Adults should have passion too. Those passions often take different forms, but they should still exist, and they should still thrive. You need to take time for your interests to let them be because by taking that time, you are letting yourself exist without judgment. You are letting yourself relax into yourself. You are teaching yourself to love who you are again.

Recognize Your Strengths

To know who you are, you need to know what you are good at. Knowing what you are good at can often confuse your idea of what you like, so be sure to differentiate the things that you are good at with the things that you like. You could like making cakes but could also be bad at baking. Your strengths can be things that you don't like just as your weaknesses can be things that you do like. You can acknowledge that you are good at filing your taxes even if you hate filing your taxes! Thus, knowing your strengths is meant to help you get to know yourself better. It is not meant to change what you enjoy!

Don't be modest about your strengths. Don't go bragging to others about them, but there's no point in being modest to yourself. Let yourself be proud. There's nothing wrong with feeling good when you do something well. Some people are raised to be modest, and this modesty sometimes converts into not feeling confident. I'm not saying that it is bad to be modest, but it's important to know the line between modesty and hating everything about yourself. You must have moments of pride, or you will never have any confidence.

Build upon your strengths. If you have certain strengths, you can use those strengths to further pursuits that you love. For example, if you are organized, you can use those skills to organize an adult recreational basketball league. You might not be the best basketball player, but you enjoy it, so you can use what you are good at to create a league that allows you to practice a hobby that you'd like to get better at. In this scenario, you have entered a win-win situation, and you have allowed yourself the chance you need to be true to yourself through existing skills.

Don't belittle your strengths. There's no need to say, "I'm good at, but," or to downplay what you're good at in any other way. Come on; you deserve better than that. Stop adding caveats and own up to your skill. You don't have to be the best at something to say that you are good at it. My eighty-year-old father isn't Michael Jordan, but for an eight-year-old, he still plays basketball pretty well! Other people's skills don't reduce your own. What comes easily for one person is harder for you, so getting a free throw may be an accomplishment for you, but it might be simple for someone else. Your skills shouldn't be compared to others. You can be impressed by personal accomplishments just because of all the work and care you put in to get where you are.

Your strengths should be parts of yourself that you can lean on when you are struggling with your self-esteem. They should not fully fuel your self-esteem, but they are good when you need self-esteem. Knowing your strengths, allows you to see the good in yourself. It shows you that you are worth the space that you take up. You may not be the best at something, but being able to push forward and work on your skills says a lot about you as a person.

Determine Your Weaknesses

Your weaknesses are nearly as important as your strengths, but not in the way that you may think. No one likes to look too closely at their weaknesses, but you need to if you want to be honest about who you are. Your weaknesses are part of yourself, but I want you to avoid shaming or judging yourself for your weaknesses. You can improve your weaknesses, but you will never do that by trying to deny them or ignore them. You need to accept that you are not perfect, and you will never be perfect (nor would you want to be).

Figure out what your weaknesses are. This first step should be pretty obvious, but it is still important. You need to know what your weaknesses are, which is not as easy as it sounds. Dig deeper than "I am bad at golf." What makes you bad at golf? Your lack of practice? A lack of muscle strength? A lack of concentration? Don't just think of things you can't do, figure out what makes it hard for you to do well at those things. Maybe you struggle at work because you are impulsive. Acknowledging that is much more helpful than saying simply, "I suck at my job."

Determine how your weaknesses impact you. You've already started to do this with the previous step, but continue to evaluate how your weakness impacts your life in multiple ways. Let's go back to the struggling at work example. Do your work problems go beyond just work? What else does that weak area influence? Does your hardship at work make you stressed? Does the stress cause you to get frustrated with your spouse more easily? Does your frustration with your spouse lead to marital issues? Think of the chain reaction of your weaknesses so you can see the more elaborate ways that they impact your life. By knowing all this information, you can more easily see the roots and pluck them out.

Know how to undermine your weaknesses. Once you have found all the associations that your weaknesses have, you can start to undermine them. You can find ways to resist those weaknesses. If you're impulsive, for example, you can learn techniques that insist that you count before you act so that you respond to situations more mindfully. If you are exhausted and act irritable with your loved ones, you can take steps to improve your sleep schedule and patterns. For whatever weaknesses you have, there are ways to ameliorate those weaknesses. Some weaknesses you can get rid of altogether, but even the ones you can't get rid of, you can improve.

Your weaknesses aren't going to destroy you if you don't let them. You are not a Greek tragedy. You don't have to have a fatal flaw. Weaknesses don't have to be something that you hate about yourself. You can use them to learn who you are and to improve your situation. Awareness is the key to having control over something, so when you can have a close connection to your weaknesses, those weaknesses won't blindside you.

Case Study: Marion and Elena

Marion was a seventy-three-year-old widow, who still didn't know who she was after the death of her husband five years prior. Her whole world had shifted. She was once the guardian of her now grown twenty-three-year-old granddaughter, Elena, who had self-esteem issues of her own to address, which would come to overlap with Marion's. There was half a century between the women, but they were more alike than they were different, and they each had similarly negative relationships with themselves. They'd soon bond over their hardships, and they would learn how important it is to know who you are and to embrace that person.

Marion had worked hard all her life, but now that she was retired, her husband was dead, and her granddaughter was grown, she wasn't sure where to go next. Her life went from being so busy to having little going on. She was restless, and she couldn't think of anything that she truly enjoyed. She had friends, but most of them were busy with lives of their own. Some were dead. Her closest friend had moved away to Florida, and Marion called her, and even video called her, but it wasn't the same as being near her. Marion missed the old days, but she didn't want to give up on her future. She had come to rely on having people around, and then, they were gone.

Elena, meanwhile, was at the age that she was starting to feel too old for certain interests. With her new job, she wanted a fresh start, and she wanted to "finally be a real adult." Nevertheless, her new job paid less than twenty thousand a year, and Elena had student debts to pay off not to mention a desire to go back to school for her masters in social work. She wanted to renounce all childish things and have independence because that's what felt most mature to her, but her salary wasn't making it easy to pay all her expenses, so she wound up moving back in with her grandmother until she could whittle down some of her debts. Elena felt like a failure despite doing everything that she was supposed to do.

Marion thought it was nice to have Elena back home, but their dynamic was different. Elena was older now and needed independence. She even insisted on paying a small rent and chipping in for other expenses. Marion wouldn't have demanded that, but Elena, wanting to have some semblance of independence, insisted. Elena couldn't thank her grandmother enough for all she had done for her. When Elena's parents died, she had been little, but her grandparents had raised her even though they felt too old and tired for a little one. The two women learned to endure their new dynamics, and they both liked the fact that they weren't alone, but there was still a gap in both their lives. They felt like they weren't being true to themselves, and they weren't. They were going through the motions without committing to themselves and their interests.

Marion found herself avoiding all the things that she used to do with her husband. Even grocery shopping was something she dreaded because she used to do that with Paul every Sunday. Whenever she could, she sent Elena instead. Marion stayed inside most days, and she knew that if she didn't start getting more active that her health would suffer. She'd never been the type to sit around. Even so, for the life of her, she didn't know what to do with herself. It felt like a limb had been chopped off and that she had no help determining how to live without it. She looked in the mirror and felt that a huge part of her was gone.

Elena had a secret, one that she had never admitted to anyone. She was a fan of a teen heartthrob, who had been part of a boyband and was now doing solo work. He was her guilty pleasure. She had a secret fan account for him on social media, and she would follow his career closely, never missing an interview. She felt silly and ashamed for being so into an artist when she was nearly twenty-four. She'd thought she'd outgrow her obsession after high school, but it had followed her into college, and it persisted even when she'd graduated college. When anyone asked her what she liked, Elena would make up other interests, and the more she hid her love for her secret pop star, the more detached from herself Elena felt.

Her interest was harming anyone. There wasn't anything wrong with it, but Elena started to feel like there was something wrong with her. So, she deleted her accounts, and she tried to make her interest in the pop star go away. She threw his posters and magazines away. She tried to stop herself from listening to his music. She tried not to pay attention to news stories about him. She ran away from something that gave her joy because she didn't want to admit her interest to other people. She pretended her pop star didn't exist, which was hard because he seemed to be everywhere. She felt awful when she didn't buy tickets for his world tour, but she forced herself to have "better" interests. She tried to like more mature artists, and some of them she enjoyed, but she missed her pop star.

That Christmas, under the glistening of a six-foot artificial Christmas tree that Marion and Elena had decorated with old ornaments, Marion had wrapped two concert tickets to the pop star's show. Elena opened them, and she froze. She didn't know how to respond. She felt a rush of joy seeing the tickets, but she also didn't want to fall back into her "immature" obsession. She wanted to defend herself and say that she wasn't interested in him anymore, but the look on Marion's face, joy that she could give her granddaughter something nice, wasn't something Elena wanted to ruin because Marion hadn't been that happy in quite a while. Elena gave her thanks, but the tickets felt heavy in her hand. One concert wouldn't hurt, she figured, but who would she bring? None of her friends knew that she still liked the pop star, and she didn't want to admit to them that she did.

Having no one else to go with, Elena sheepishly smiled at her grandma and said, "Do you want to go with me?"

Marion looked surprised, and she waved the suggestion away. She felt too old to be going to a concert with her granddaughter, especially one for an artist who was "for young people." She hadn't been to a concert since when Elena was a teenager and needed an adult chaperone to see the boyband the pop star had been a part of.

Elena cajoled her, "Come on, it will be fun," and the idea was growing on Elena. Her grandmother wouldn't have been her first pick for a concert buddy, but they'd not had a lot of time together, so it would be nice, and Elena wouldn't feel like she had to hide. The pop star's music wasn't her grandmother's style, but Elena knew it had been a while since her grandmother had gone out and done something interesting. She thought it might be good for Marion to push past her comfort zone. Elena could see that Marion wasn't doing well, and maybe spending some time together could be fun. Marion had always loved concerts when she was young, but she had long ago waved them off as being impractical.

After some debate, Marion relented reluctantly. It wasn't like she had much else to do. She was old, not an invalid, and she was sure that she could handle one concert, even one with thousands of screaming young women. It had been so long since she had done something just for fun without any other practical purpose, so the promise of doing something so new and interesting appealed to Marion. It would give her a taste of all the activities that she had lost in her youth. She'd heard some of the pop star's songs on the radio too, and she had to admit that she didn't mind them.

Elena and Marion both felt a weight lifted when they went to the concert. They both felt a little insecure at first, but they felt the tension leave their shoulders as they listened to the music. While the concert didn't automatically fix everything, it didn't promote change in both women's lives. Elena realized that in denying her interests, she was denying herself, and Marion realized that there were things in life that she could love without her husband. She and Elena have been to several concerts since the first one. Some of them were Elena's choice while others were for musical groups that Marion loved.

CHAPTER 6
Stop Trying To Be Someone You Aren't

Know When You're Trying to Please Others

When you try to please others, you are neglecting yourself. You're trying to be the person who other people want you to be, and that person isn't you. Trying to please others drains you of your wants. It makes you feel obligated to do certain things that you wouldn't otherwise have any reason to do. Trying to please others is often a crutch. It allows you to have a life with some direction, but it doesn't force you to go through the hard work of getting to know yourself. Pleasing others can give you a quick burst of confidence, but it is not the key to long-term self-esteem. Satisfaction based on the wants of others is short-lived, so true self-esteem has to come from within.

Figure out the situations that cause you to bend to other people's wills. Everyone has triggers that make them want to 'people please'. Some have more than others. Whenever you find that you are trying to please others at the expense of yourself, make a note. As the notes build, you may start to see some trends leap out. If you don't, look harder, and try to see if any patterns emerge. Do you try to please your mother? Do you overcompensate to please your boss after you've made a mistake? What is it that sends you into people-pleasing-mode? When you start to see patterns, you can be better prepared to fight against your actions.

Be able to catch yourself in the act. Once you know the causes of your people-pleasing, you can start to catch yourself in the act. You can make the unconscious behaviors conscious, and you can say, "Hey, I'm feeling anxious about my job right now, so that explains why I'm pushing myself past my limits to try to make my boss happy." You can start to see when you need to take a step back and recollect yourself. You'll be able to start figuring out when you need to take time to attend to your own needs. You can't do good work if you are neglecting yourself. To succeed at anything, self-care is necessary, so keep that in mind when you're trying to make other people happy. You'll make them happier if you are taken care of.

Don't do anything that compromises your core values. If something goes against one of your core values, you don't need to do it. Compromising those values that are foundational to you will only make you feel worse about yourself. Sometimes, you'll be put in a hard position where you may have to compromise some of your values to survive (like taking a job with an organization you don't believe in), but never compromise your values merely to make someone else happy (and try not to compromise them at all). If you don't feel comfortable doing something, be communicative. There's nothing wrong with telling your boss or spouse that you don't feel right with something that you are expected to do. Handle it maturely and see if you can find a solution that pleases everyone. Your mental and physical health shouldn't be compromised in the process!

There's nothing wrong with wanting to make other people happy, but you can't neglect the need to make yourself happy. If you focus too much on other people's needs, you may let their wants consume you. Your personality may get intertwined with theirs to the point that you forget what you like and what you want. This loss of identity that you face is one of the most harmful side-effects of being a people pleaser. People pleasers rely on other people to feel good about themselves, but it is not healthy to rely so heavily on other people for a feeling of confidence. You have to feel confident all on your own.

No One Likes A Faker

The truth is that no one likes it when people aren't genuine. If you try to be someone who you aren't, you can't also be yourself. If you are a faker, you aren't going to get very far in life. You may get a semblance of success, but do you ever really have success if you can't own up to yourself? Not really. If you can't succeed being yourself, then that success isn't fulfilling. When you succeed trying to be someone else, you sell yourself out, and you convince the people around you that a person who doesn't truly exist is you!

When you aren't genuine, you won't make strong relationships. People can often see through your guise. They may not always know it consciously, but people can often sense that you are not being honest with them. They can feel that there is a lack of deep connection. You may say a lot, but if you aren't being genuine, you're dancing around things that make you most passionate. I can easily tell when people are hiding behind facades, and I have also learned to tell when I am putting facades up to protect myself from hurt. As you start to be more genuine and open, you'll be able to have a better sense of this as well.

You may start to isolate yourself if you feel like you need to hide your true self. People who hide themselves are often lonely. It doesn't matter if they spend all their time surrounded by people. They feel lonely if they can't share who they really are because they are avoiding intimacy. You cannot be emotionally intimate if you don't share who you are, and that lack of intimacy can be felt by both you and the people around you. You end up feeling like no one understands you the way that you want them to. You want to be known, we all do, but if you have low self-esteem and aren't genuine, you can never be known how you deserve to be known, in the important way that touches the soul so deeply.

Faking who you are won't get you anywhere. It's not going to make you happier. It's just going to make you feel alone and alienate you from many potentially strong relationships. Nobody likes a faker, yourself included. If you felt that someone was hiding something from you, you wouldn't want to be vulnerable with that person because it would feel too dangerous. You need to be vulnerable for vulnerability to be returned. That vulnerability will give you the strong relationships that you need, to be honest about who you are and to feel good about yourself.

Love What You Can't Change

Loving what you can't change is one of the most important messages in this entire book, so if you learn nothing else, learn this because you need to accept that there are things that aren't perfect that you will still have to love. You'll have to love them because they are part of you. They are yours, and so if you don't tend to them with care and compassion, no one else will. If you reject them, so will everyone else. You need to take the first step and love all the things about yourself that other people won't necessarily accept or understand.

Love your flaws. It doesn't matter what those flaws are, you need to find ways to love them. Loving them doesn't mean that you don't want to improve them. You can want to improve something without hating it. I love my mother, but I still want her to quit smoking. You can have respect for qualities that you have without losing accountability for your behaviors. You can love your anger for a feeling that you have, but throwing a brick at some because you're angry isn't acceptable! Love your anger because it is part of your passion. It is part of the fuel you've used to get where you are. It's not a feeling you want to have all the time, but it is a feeling you have, and that's okay.

Love your body. Your body is an incredible machine. Even if you have disabilities or limitations that others don't have, it's still amazing that you are alive. The fact that you are breathing is a wonderful feat. Your body keeps you alive, and you don't even have to consciously think of staying alive to stay alive. Your body takes care of that for you, which is so cool. Think about all the things that your body can do rather than all the things that it can't do. Embrace your body for its acts rather than its looks as well. Who cares what you look like. Your body is a vessel that you can use to do incredible things and express yourself. Your looks are an expression of your DNA. They are who you are, and that's nothing to be ashamed of.

Love your mind. Your mind is strong. No matter how high or low your IQ, your mind keeps your body functioning. It allows you to read this book. It allows you to laugh and smile. It allows you to know yourself. Your mind has unique gifts that no one else has. It is all yours, and it is something that you should cherish for all it does to help you. Your mind is not inherently wrong. You're not evil if you have bad thoughts. The best people still have bad thoughts. It is your actions that define you, and your brain can do so many good reactions.

Love uniqueness. You're not like other people, and why would you want to be. Your uniqueness is what makes you able to do things that other people can't. It is what differentiates you from all the other people in the world. Don't run away from what makes you happy because you're afraid of all that makes you special. Don't feel embarrassed about your uniqueness. Embrace it because there's no sense trying to be anyone else. Anyone else isn't going to make you feel genuine. It won't give you a reason to feel about yourself. The adage, "Be yourself because everyone else is taken," is accurate.

You have to love yourself, not the person you wish you were. Love yourself right now. Don't wait until you've lost weight, gotten a promotion, or found someone to marry. You can't wait to love yourself. There's never a better time to start loving yourself because you'll always have excuses about why you can't love yourself. Love yourself right now. Don't delay the happiness that can derive from self-love.

You're Worthy Just as You Are

Even if you could change yourself, you don't need to. Right now, you are worthy of good things and happiness. You don't need to earn your worth. It's inherent in you, and it is waiting for you to embrace it. Don't doubt that you deserve to be treated as well as you are. You don't have to be someone else to be worthy. You don't have to be perfect. You don't have to please other people. You are worth it, and if you can believe that, the whole world will have no choice but to think that it is true because your worth mostly depends on the worth you give yourself.

You deserve to be treated properly by others. I don't care what you've done in your past. I don't care if you've made mistakes. People shouldn't treat you like you are nothing. You are something, and as long as you are trying to be someone good, you deserve all the respect in the world. You don't have to wait until you've made all your amends. You don't have to keep beating yourself up over your mistakes. Pay the cost of the wrongs you have done, but don't continue to self-flagellate for the rest of your life. Most people don't do things that are that horrific that they deserve only hate.

You are worth being fully yourself. You shouldn't have to hide parts of yourself based on who you are with. In an ideal world, you would be able to show whatever parts you want of yourself at any time. You would be able to fully show who you are without being hurt or rejected by others. Unfortunately, people do hurt others for what they don't understand, but that doesn't mean that you don't deserve to be yourself. You do. You deserve that as much as anyone else. People will always be prejudiced, but that prejudice isn't deserved. Prejudice is a result of other people's insecurities and their misplaced attempts at feeling confident. It is not your fault, but unfortunately, it is your problem.

While you can always improve and be a better version of yourself, you will always be yourself. You're the person that you will be stuck with for the rest of your life, so you better find ways to be who you are. Don't try to be someone else to make other people happy or to run away from parts of yourself that you are afraid of. You are worth more than running scared. You deserve to come face to face with yourself and say, "I am worth the space that I take up. I deserve life and happiness. I should be my whole self." Keep repeating that message until you believe it because you have value as a human, and no one should be able to make you feel like you don't.

Case Study: Andrea and Devon

Andrea and Devon's fear of being themselves nearly cost them their marriage before they were able to right the dysfunction and lack of confidence that had struck them.

Andrea and Devon were a couple I met while doing business in upstate New York. They were one of the few black couples in the neighborhood that they moved into, which set them apart further from the people around them. From the moment they drove into their cul-de-sac, they felt like aliens from an unknown planet. They tried to assure themselves that they belonged. They told themselves that they worked hard to get where they were, but despite all the failed affirmations, they still felt like imposters. They felt unwelcomed despite all the neighbors having been, for the most part, friendly. Some were racists and would treat Andrea and Devon with microaggressions, which only made them feel more like outsiders in their community.

Andrea was a teacher, and Devon was a doctor. They'd both grown up poor, so as Devon started to earn heaps of money when he finished school and rose through the ranks at his hospital, they were thrust into wealthy circles that they couldn't navigate. Again, they felt like they were on the outside looking again. They weren't used to upper-class events, so it took many uncomfortable experiences to learn how people used to money behaved. They were more frugal with their money than most others, and they weren't showy. Andrea felt like a freak when a female doctor, married to another doctor, rudely commented about Andrea repeating outfits.

As a teacher, Andrea didn't make as much as her husband, and she'd go to events with doctor's wives, who sometimes didn't work at all, and she felt like a pauper merely pretending to be someone of importance. She'd fidget at the events, feeling as though everyone was judging her for one thing or another. Logically, she knew that most of the people were nice, but the thought that they weren't kept her from sharing too much about herself. She grew quiet and tried not to be her usually bubbly self because she'd been told in the past that she was "too loud." Devon felt equally apprehensive. He was a doctor, but he still felt like a kid with five siblings living in a small New York City apartment. He didn't understand all the lingo or the politics among the socialites in upstate New York, and he didn't get why appearances mattered so much.

Neither realized that the other was struggling, but the friction was tangible. The couple both had pent up anxiety that they couldn't seem to release, and they each felt like they couldn't fit in. Devon started putting more hours into work, and Andrea resented that secretly because she felt even more separated from that world the more Devon was apart from her. She would come from work at around three, and she'd be along for much of the afternoon and evening. She hadn't made many friends, and she wasn't willing to be emotionally vulnerable to try to expand her small social circle. She was from a small town in California, so small-town New York was foreign to her, and she felt so far away from her loved ones that she ached.

Andrea and Devon both were unhappy about having to act the part of an upper-class couple, but their charade wasn't necessary. They were pretending because they were afraid of being themselves, but when they decided that they needed to make changes, they realized that Devon's coworkers weren't as intimidating as they thought.

It turns out that there were several people in the group of doctors who came from backgrounds not that far off from Devon and Andrea's, and as they challenged themselves to get to know people better, they realized that they weren't outsiders after all. They were able to be vulnerable and share themselves in ways that eased some of the tension they felt. Devon and Andrea were relieved to not have to pretend anymore. Their marriage still needed work to make it function healthily again. Andrea and Devon were able to improve their relationship and establish a healthy group of friends, including some of Devon's colleagues. They now have two little girls. It's less work for them now to feel confident in upper-class circles. They still feel humble, but they don't feel as overwhelmed by their community.

CHAPTER 7
Let Go Of The Opinions Of Others

Other People Don't Know Your Perspective

At the end of the day, no one knows everything that you've been through. Even you can't remember everything about yourself, so no matter how well-intended people's opinions of you are, they aren't going to be complete. Thus, you cannot take them at face value. You cannot assume that what a person says about you is true just as you cannot read one shady blog post and take that as fact. Much of the hardship we have with our identity with ourselves is fueled by the way that other people see us, though, which makes it so vital for us to understand our relationships with ourselves and how opinions influence that relationship.

While people can try to empathize, we can't fully understand what it is like to be other people. Empathy allows us to know what it would be like to be other people in a very limited manner. Based on our past experiences, we can surmise how they might feel. We can feel a small bit of their feelings by knowing what it is like to be human, but we can never know the full breadth of someone else's feelings or their personality. They cannot share everything with us, and we will never interpret it the same way that they do. All we can do is *try* to understand others. Thus, don't expect that other people can know you better than yourself. Even if you are denying yourself or repressing who you are, you have the best information on you. All you have to do is use it.

People will project their own experiences onto you. It is inevitable that people's opinions on others will be formed by what they've experienced before. Thus, your boyfriend may have been cheated on before, and he assumes that when you're talking to another man that you are cheating. He forms the opinion that you are doing something wrong. He may try to make you think that you are doing something wrong. That would be abusive behavior, but it happens, nevertheless. Don't let other people convince you that you are wrong. Sometimes, people are so good at manipulation that it can be hard to see that you are being manipulated and used but resist as much as you can and check-in with yourself to ensure that other people's opinions aren't changing your sense of self. If your sense of self is changing, especially because of a relationship, that's a warning sign that something is wrong.

Some people will try hard to understand you, and they will have good intentions, but they will not fully get you. That's how humans are. Sometimes, there will be malicious intentions, but mostly, people are trying their best to help you. Even so, their attempts can mess with your head and make you question who you are. They can make you think that you are a different person, which will never lead to self-confidence. To be confident, you have to put your opinion of yourself above other people's opinions of you. To do this, you need to believe in your value as a person outside how other people value you.

Stop Internalizing Bad Messages

When people tell you things that they don't like about you, it's easy to take that negativity inside ourselves and make it ours. You take biases that other people have, and you bring them within yourself, which decreases your self-esteem. For most prejudices, there is a corresponding internalization— internalized homophobia, internalized racism, internalized misogyny, etc. What you are can be something that you have a deep hate for without even knowing it. These internalized feelings do some of the most harm and can be the hardest to break through. Nevertheless, you can combat them and ensure that they don't drive your life.

People often grow to hate people like them due to low self-esteem. They internalize the negativity around them, and they start to repress themselves and think that they are bad. It is unfortunate when people use the hate that is given to them to further hate against themselves and others. Internalized hate spreads just like any other hate, so one person who has internalized negative messages may then spread those same messages to other people who will internalize them. This situation makes for a lot of unnecessary pain that could be prevented with a little kindness and understanding. Too often, society makes judgments without understanding why.

Society is going to try to make you feel like you are wrong; you aren't wrong. For anyone who doesn't fit molds, society will try to convince you that parts of yourself aren't acceptable. Those parts of yourself aren't wrong. You aren't wrong for existing or being yourself. You deserve to have individuality, which is why you need to confront the conformity that society pushes. You need to ask yourself if societal norms are true or if they are more malicious. Be critical with the things that you feel are expected and learn to think for yourself rather than relying on the opinions of everyone else.

Avoid letting those bad messages alter your view of yourself by knowing what you believe in. Know what your views are so that you can't be easily swayed by other views. Put your values first. If you believe in treating people equally, don't stand for actions that will interfere with that value. Don't say, "equality is for everyone but..." because that allows room for saying that somehow people like you might not deserve that equality, but you do. Your values assert that you do, so stick to those values. It's okay to invalidate values over time when you realize that they are harmful, but if your values aren't harmful, there's no reason to get rid of them.

Know how to spot internalized messages. Learn when you really think something about yourself versus what you are repeating that others have said about you. Distinguishing these ideas is vital to your well-being because it ensures that you are not internalizing messages that will make you feel insecure. The more you practice separating the messages that you receive, the easier it will be to deal with your internalized negativity, and the more confident you will feel.

Other People Can't Define You

You are never defined by what other people think of you because they can never know you as you know yourself. People can't define you if you don't let them, so don't let them. Tell yourself that you know who you are, and be confident in your analysis of yourself. Of course, you're going to be biased, but you're also going to feel better about yourself. You are going to feel worthy and confident, and when you feel those things, you'll be better able to consider other people's opinions of you without feeling that you are being attacked. You'll take constructive criticism without feeling that it is the end of the world, which leads to genuine growth and happiness.

People's opinions of you are not always rooted in logic. When people have an opinion of you, they aren't going to have any grounding in reality. Sometimes, they will say things merely to be nasty, or they will say them to hit a point of insecurity. Other people often will target your insecurities to throw you off guard, and they don't care if those insecurities are valid or not. As long as those insecurities can disarm you, they are a weapon, but if you can get control of those insecurities via confidence, the insecurities won't go away fully, but you'll be able to manage them. People will be able to insult you and you won't automatically accept what they are saying as truth.

Remember that no matter what people think of you, you can define yourself however you want. If you want to be a team-player, start acting like a team player using the skills you already have. If you want to be a parent, take steps to be a parent. You get to choose how your personality correlates to your identity. While you cannot change your personality, you get to decide how you shape your identity. Identity is a fluid concept, meaning you can shift it and look at it through whatever lens you would like.

You Can Resist Other People's Opinions

Other people's opinions will always be there to remind you how others feel about you. They will bombard you. They will catch you off guard. Often, they will sour your mood. To some extent, these negative feelings of criticism cannot be avoided. They are part of being human, but they do not have to be weaknesses. They don't have to paralyze your ability function. Other people's opinions don't have to change the course that you are on. They don't have to make you feel like you want to be a completely different person.

You don't have to take everything that other people say to heart.

Sometimes, good people or people who you love deeply will have prejudices that hurt you. It's usually the worst when people you love give unsatisfactory opinions. When your mother gives an opinion, for example, you may feel especially vulnerable. You may feel like you've been reduced to being a little kid who broke your mother's favorite vase. Remember that you're not that little kid anymore. You don't need to feel like you did then. You can bounce back from that criticism. It doesn't have to be an attack on your entire sense of self.

No matter how hard you try to please people, you can't escape opinions. Some opinions will be good, but it's so much easier to hold onto the bad. We fixate on the bad things that are said about us sometimes to the point of insanity. Try holding onto the good opinions instead. Let them validate the good feelings that you have about yourself. The bad feelings that you have about yourself don't need any encouragement. They like to run wild no matter what. The good ones are shyer and sometimes require some coaxing to get them to come to the forefront of your mind.

Case Study: Jessie

Jessie always let the opinions of others get to him. Someone would tell him something about himself, and he would easily agree to whatever they said. His self-esteem was so low that he always assumed that he had to be the one in the wrong. At work, he'd work on projects with groups, and he wouldn't assert himself. When someone made a mistake, he wouldn't question them because he'd assume that he must have been the one who was mistaken. His self-doubt made it hard for him to function and be his best self. He felt like he was fading and becoming a shell of a person, and he knew that something had to change. If it didn't, he'd never emerge from the self-hating funk that had followed him from childhood.

Jessie grew up as an only child in a middle-class family. His mother was critical to her one son. She signed him up for a weight loss program when he was six, and she would monitor his diet closely. He wasn't even considered overweight at that time, but he was close to that level, and he was bigger than the other kids, which bothered his mother. She was sure that he would be obese by the time he was in middle school, and she was right, but many of Jessie's food issues were provoked by his mother's treatment of him in those early years. He craved "forbidden" foods more when he wasn't allowed to have them, and he started to eat them in secret whenever he could. He packed on the weight, and his mom kept finding him more diets that didn't work.

Although Jessie knew that his mother meant well, the pain of his early battle with his weight followed him, and he still is sensitive to criticism because of how relentless he felt his mother's criticism was. For all her faults, his mother loved him deeply, and when he would later come out as gay, she accepted him with no sign of disappointment. Being gay was hard for Jessie, but he said that it was never as bad as being fat.

When he was in high school, it was common for kids to use "gay" and "fat" as insults rather than as descriptors. Jessie was both, and he struggled to accept who he was. He felt like an abomination. He lived in a liberal area, so most people were accepting, but the kids in his school tried to make him feel bad merely because they could. They were using the words that they knew would bother him the most, and their taunts made Jessie feel deplorable. He wanted to feel better, but he felt like nothing would ever save him from the awful feelings that consumed him. Jessie started to think that he was the worst person in the world. Other people's criticisms would make Jessie lose his head. Every insult felt like the end of the world, and Jessie didn't have enough confidence to rationalize the abusive comments away. They didn't go in one ear and out the other. They went in one ear and got caught, stuck in the lobes of his brain. He'd ruminate for hours sometimes, and the thoughts made him want to stay in his bed forever.

Even out of high school, people constantly bombarded Jessie with comments about how bad it was that he was fat. Occasionally, they would insult him for being gay. He was so sick of two qualities that caused so much grief from other people. He hated that people were so opinionated about his identity, but he still had all the internalized homophobia and fatphobia that he hadn't worked through.

By the time he was forty, Jessie was fatter than ever, and he hadn't had a serious relationship in years. He wanted a deeper connection, but it didn't feel like that was ever going to happen. He felt like the worst person alive, and he wished that he could change his fatness. Sometimes, he even wished that he could change his gayness. He even hated himself for the fact that he had bought into the negative messages that other people had thrown his way. He wished that he could be more resistant to them, but he felt so depleted that he couldn't defend himself from the attacks on his character.

It wasn't until his mom died that Jessie realized he had never gotten to be a person he liked. He felt sad that he would never make his mom proud. He wanted to do something to get his life back in order before he too died. He needed to do something if he didn't want to feel like an abomination forever.

Jessie had let the opinions of others kill the spark in his eyes. He wound up feeling lonely, and at times, he was suicidal. His self-esteem was at an all-time low when he reached out to a therapist and practically begged for help. He felt like he'd wasted his whole life being insecure, but he was ready to change. He wanted to feel better about himself and be able to fall in love. He couldn't fall in love when he hated himself. Today, Jessie is still working on being better, but he continues to make strides to break the chains of his low self-esteem. He thinks he will always struggle, but finally, he is willing to fight for himself, and that's the biggest step forward that anyone with self-esteem issues can take. It's a scary step, but facing your fears is an inevitable part of the process of building your self-esteem.

CHAPTER 8
Don't Let Fear Control You

How Fears Debilitate You

Fear is your body's way of keeping you safe. When you are afraid, your body is reacting to other things that have happened to you in the past. Your animalistic brain is going into fight, flight, or freeze mode. You are not thinking logically; you are defaulting to your instincts so that you can have a fast response to your threat. This is the basic way that your brain operates— when it feels in danger, it skips over conscious decisions, and you make unconscious decisions. This method is not bad. In fact, it keeps you safe. If you were at a baseball game and a ball flies at you, you would know to either catch it or duck. You wouldn't have to stop and consciously react. Your body would take over to make sure you didn't get hit by the ball. It's a protection method, but humans aren't as wild as we once were. We are not constantly under threat from scary animals and natural elements. Nevertheless, our instincts remain. These instincts can result in fear making us unable to think rationally. When that happens, our insecurities can ensure that we back away from embracing ourselves. You learn from past experiences that your doubts about yourself must be true, so you don't trust yourself to do what is right, and you make it harder for yourself to make decisions and react to intense scenarios. You stand in your own way, and in the process, you can make the doubts you have come true by not trusting yourself.

Fear makes it hard to think clearly. When you have fears, you aren't able to think rationally. Your brain gets fuzzy with terror, and you can't even process the information that is striking you. You can only rely on your instincts until your brain realizes that you are not in danger and that you have the time you need to think logically rather than instinctually. When you are nervous, you may make the wrong decisions simply because you can not calm the part of your brain, the medulla, and the hindbrain, that makes primal decisions. You are a victim of your urges, and the only way to change that is to face your fears and become in charge of them.

Fear creates narratives that aren't true. Fear makes you think that doing certain things will cause you to be in danger. It takes normal activities, and it makes them scary. It warps reality, and it convinces you that you must restrain yourself to avoid danger. It also makes you miss out on many things that would give you joy. It tells you that you will never be good enough. It convinces you that you have no worth. Fear is only as true as you allow it to be. It is an abstract thing, so it should have little sway over you, but it has so much power for many people. It's impossible to be fearless, but you can be fear resistant.

Fear causes you to be a self-fulfilling prophecy. Whenever you are afraid, you avoid certain circumstances, and the tactics you use to avoid the circumstances you fear mean that you'll never get hurt by what you fear, but they also mean that you will never succeed. If you're afraid of not getting a promotion, you might not even try for the promotion, or you might subconsciously do lesser work, so you don't even have the chance to be promoted. This behavior is self-sabotaging, but it is all too common for people with low self-esteem. The more you fear, the harder it is to try for success.

Fear does all that, and so much more. You shouldn't be afraid of the monster under your bed because it is not real. It is just fear. Fear is cowardly when you face it. It runs away and can't stand up to your calm brain, but fear can be the worst monster you face if you let it feed off your self-esteem. Keep your fear in check to avoid letting it control you. It's never too late to face your fears. Face them as soon as possible, though, because the longer you have them, the scarier it is to deal with them.

Common Fears

Often, the fears that people with low self-esteem have fall similar trends. They have the same recurring fears that haunt them and pop up constantly throughout their lives. These fears often have valid roots. They are based on past hurts that your brain wants you to avoid in the future, but your brain is overprotective, and it overblows the power of the things that you are afraid of. In the process, you suffer, and you are consumed by your anxiety. You can't believe in yourself with all the doubt clogging up your brain. It's tiring, and it's a dreadful way to live

The fear of failure is one of the most pervasive fears in society. Some studies have estimated that it is the most popular fear among the adult population. Failure is a vague fear, which makes it even more obtrusive for people who have it. It takes up every part of their life. It nags at them, and it convinces them that no matter what they try, they will not succeed. Any little success is belittled by this fear. This fear is the ultimate self-esteem breaker. It grinds down all your confidence until you feel as though you can do no right. This fear is always false.

Another common fear can take up two ends of a spectrum. Some people fear that they are not enough while others fear that they are too much. Both fears further the narrative that the person is not worthy of the space they take up. You may feel like you are too annoying and talk too loud. Alternatively, you may feel like you are the tiniest person alive and are still taking up too much space. You're not enough to deserve the tiny piece of space you take up. Again, this fear is false. You take up exactly as much space as you should when you are at your most confident. You deserve to exist and to be part of this world fully.

Fears related to money are also all too common. Many people worry about making ends meet or fear that they are not good enough providers. This fear is often valid because money is an important part of life. Without money, it is hard to survive and assure that your basic needs are met. Nevertheless, people often take this fear too far. They worry far beyond just how much money they need to survive. They compare their net worth to that of others and think that they cannot possibly measure up. They put all their value into how much they make, which makes it hard for them to feel as though they ever make enough. This fear can go beyond money itself and also include other material things. It is a fear that you don't need to have because your worth is not determined by your income or possessions.

Professional fears or fears related to accomplishing certain fears are also too prevalent. Just like people get worked up about their possessions or money, they also tend to be sensitive about their jobs or other goals. They have a plan about how much they should accomplish by a certain point, but this mindset is often harmful because it pushes an idea of success that is not accurate. Accomplishments happen at their own pace, and it shouldn't feel like a failure if you get a promotion you wanted at twenty-six instead of twenty-five. Cut yourself some slack and know that life isn't a competition. You don't have to get to the finish line first— if you do, you are dead.

People with low self-esteem often worry that they are outcasts. They feel like they don't belong among other people and that certain qualities about them make them freaks. They can be perfectly "normal" people and still insist that they are the oddest humans alive and that they don't fit in. Some people find any lack of conformity to be unnerving, even if being human means that, in some ways, we must not conform. No human can conform completely, not should they want to. Everyone is different so by being different, you are conforming to what it means to be human without conforming to the more specific objectives that society says you should follow.

Many people fear that they are imposters. This is a fear that is especially prevalent among women. Imposter syndrome is a psychological mechanism that happens when people feel insecure about their place in the world. Most commonly, it happens in professional spaces. People with imposter syndrome feel like they don't deserve the positions that they have, and they feel like they will be exposed as a fraud at any moment. They become convinced that they are just like imposters, impersonating someone who would be competent. Usually, these people are competent, but they don't feel that way, and this fear can make it hard to do their best work because they become so afraid of being exposed as frauds.

You may be afraid that you constantly let people down. When you respect people, you don't want to disappoint them, and this fear of letting people down could lead to pathological people-pleasing. You become so driven to make other people happy that you become afraid of doing anything that might upset other people. It never feels good to let people down, but you let them down more when you're too afraid to do anything.

You may also fear that people are going to abandon you. People often fear that they will be left by their loved ones if they make mistakes. People who truly love you aren't going to leave you over one mistake. One mistake is never the end of the world. People do get abandoned, and this can have a powerful impact on the psyche, but being left doesn't take away from your worth. It just happens because just like you, other people have insecurities and fears that may drive them to make improper decisions.

All these fears, and other ones, only serve to hurt you. When you let fears into your life, you open yourself up to a whole lot of pain. I'm not telling you to have no fears. That would be impossible. Fears can be healthy. What I want you to do is face your fears. Look at them and see if you can get them to go away.

How to Challenge Your Fears

Challenging your fears is a great step towards gaining self-esteem. It isn't comfortable to challenge your fears, but when you do it, you will be rewarded with new opportunities and improved confidence.

Ask yourself what you are really afraid of. Consider what it is that terrifies you the most, the source of all fear. Address the root causes of your fears. Think back to the chapter on facing your trauma. If you can handle your past, you can better understand why fear plays a role in your life. Fear is rooted in past experiences.

Think about all that you risk when you let the fear go unaddressed.

Know that exposing your fears as the monsters that they are is the best way to overcome those fears. Think of all the things that fear prohibits you from doing. Ask yourself if you want to continue not doing those things. If the answer is no, then you need to challenge your fears, or you'll never do what you want to do.

Don't disregard your fears. Listen to them, but don't let them be the sole controller of your life. Fears are trying to speak to you. Let them speak, but don't let their panic influence you. Stay calm in the face of fear so that you can come out ahead.

Think of ways that what you fear is wrong. Tell yourself that you don't need to be afraid. Remind yourself that being crippled by fear will never help you accomplish anything. Find ways to defy your fear. Being defiant can be liberating, and it makes you feel bolder even if you aren't.

Challenge yourself to be courageous. Courage doesn't mean doing crazy things. It doesn't mean jumping from a plane or ducking from bullets that are flying at you as if you were an action movie character. Being brave means something different for everyone. You need to escape the trap of fear. Fear should never control you. It should guide you and help you keep yourself safe, but it shouldn't debilitate you.

Case Study: Nix

Nix grew up in a small town. They knew from an early age that they didn't belong. They didn't feel like either he or she, but they didn't know how to describe that feeling early on, so they used a pronoun that didn't feel right. Nix felt like an outsider from the beginner, but when they were young, it felt like a good thing. It was fun being different from other kids and being unique. When Nix was little, they wore dresses, but they also loved to wear Spiderman costumes, running around the house pretending to shoot webs from their hands. Nix felt unlimited and was free to express themself as they pleased.

Like many kids, Nix started their life full of energy and not at all insecure. As Nix grew older, they realized that they weren't like the other kids, but this time, they realized that it might be in a bad way. People often didn't understand Nix. They would make discomforting comments that made Nix wonder if they were not right somehow. Throughout their life, Nix couldn't conform, but they tried when they realized that people might not accept them.

Nix was good at school, athletic, and bright-eyed, but when middle school came along, Nix started to retreat from their peers. Nix was shy, and other kids would insult them. By the time Nix was in high school, they were smoking too much weed, drinking too much, and having sex too much— the trifecta of being an outsider at Nix's strict Christian school. The other kids at Nix's kids participated in those same activities, but they kept their actions hidden while gossiping about Nix's.

Despite the nature of their peers, Nix thrived in high school. They found online communities that allowed them to discover more about their gender and sexuality. While Nix was content in their internet world, Nix was still terrified of coming out to people as non-binary and pansexual. They were sure that they were going to be scrutinized. Nix grew depressed, and their life started to crumble as they grappled with who they were.

It wasn't until their freshman year in college that Nix was able to gather the courage to be themself. It was out of necessity more than anything. Nix knew that they would never be happy if they didn't take the chance on their well-being.

Nix did come against some people who didn't understand them. They were from a town where conformity was still admired. Nevertheless, Nix was able to feel confident despite the negativity. The negativity still hurt, but it didn't destroy Nix's confidence like it could have. Nix was able to face their fears of rejection to be able to come out to the world as who they were rather than continuing to unhappily hide.

CHAPTER 9
Embrace Who You Want To Be

You Can't Change Who You Inherently Are

Who you are has been well-established. Your personality isn't something that you can will to be different. If you could, confidence would be easy. If people could be whoever they wanted to be, they would all be content in themselves. They wouldn't have to face any doubt. They could embrace themselves easily when it normally is so hard. You can't just snap your fingers and love yourself, though. You can't look in the mirror and see through your self-hate. There's a fog that you must clear, wiping all the fuzziness away until your true self emerges.

Don't try to strip yourself of all the things that you hate. It is useless to try to get rid of the qualities that you don't like. You can try all you want, but the things that you don't like about yourself aren't going to go away. They are part of you, and you can choose what you do with them, but you can't decide whether they are there. Many of your qualities are built into your DNA, and you can't erase your DNA without unraveling everything that you are. It's pointless to try to fight parts of yourself that will always win.

The more you try to change, the worst you will feel about yourself. The more you try to fight yourself, the more of an enemy you will become. Some people fight themselves their entire lives. They hate themselves by the end. They aren't happy. They wish they could be happy, but no matter what they do, they can't see past their hate. They become consumed by the things that they have no power over. It's senseless, and it's demoralizing. That hate you feel about yourself isn't going to do anything for you. It will slowly kill your soul, and then you'll die feeling like a vacant version of yourself.

If you are trying to change what is inherent, you are asserting that you hate yourself, so you can never feel confident. Your brain believes the things that you tell it the most, so if you send it messages that convince it that you hate yourself, you're going to hate yourself. You'll keep believing that you hate yourself until you take strides to change that relationship that you have with yourself. The sooner you can change it the better. The purpose of self-improvement isn't to change yourself. It is to change your attitudes.

You are who you are, and there's no sense trying to fight that person. A lifetime of war never leads to peace. If you want your body and mind to be calm, you have to stop instigating a fight. Stop putting your brain on the edge. Stop trying to manipulate yourself into a person you might like better. If you can't like yourself as you were born, you can't like yourself at all. It may scare you to think that you might live the rest of your life with low self-confidence, but you can change your attitude. Your attitude is easy to change when you put in the effort and relinquish the desire to change who you fundamentally are.

You Can Change How You Look at Yourself

You don't have to look in the mirror and hate yourself. Imagine looking in the mirror and seeing someone who makes you excited. Imagine seeing a person who you think is the most beautiful in the world. Imagine that you feel no resentment towards that person. Imagine that you are free from all the stigma that you've placed on yourself. That is confidence. That is taking your low self-esteem and telling it that it has no place in your body or in your mind.

Start finding your redeeming qualities redeemable. Everyone has beauty because we are all alive and doing our best to do incredible things. The fact that you are alive and reading a book is itself remarkable. If you want to, you can start looking in the mirror and seeing someone who you love. Start by finding just a few qualities that you love, and build that up until you can love everything about yourself. If you find new qualities to appreciate each day, you will be well on the path of success and self-love.

You Can Change How You Look at the World

The way you look at things influences how you interact with your world, which correlates to how you see yourself. Your worldview inevitably is interrelated with your self-view. How you view the world is often a macrocosm for how you view yourself, so if you're struggling to improve the way you look at yourself, start by analyzing and addressing how you look at yourself. Keep a journal logging your observations about everything around you, and see what areas you look at with negativity. Then, see how that attitude negatively impacts your self-esteem and self-image. When you complete this exercise, you'll probably see that you were surprisingly negative.

You can become more positive with your outlook on life to improve your self-image. Practicing being grateful for what you have is one method that helps you be more positive. Further, you should address your treatment of others. Don't be super critical of others because if you hold other people to too high standards, you're going to hold yourself to even worse standards. If you can look upon the world with more positivity, you can look at yourself with more positivity as well. The more you practice being positive, the better off you will be. When you look at the world in new ways, you can look at yourself in new ways, so dare to see the world from a brighter perspective. Pessimism is never going to help you feel better about yourself because it makes your expectations unrealistic, and it makes it hard to see the good in the world and yourself.

You Can Change Your Confidence

You can understand what makes you insecure and what makes you afraid, and you can challenge these stressors. There are so many factors that are related to low self-esteem, and they have been interwoven throughout this book. It is these factors that are the key to unlocking your self-confidence and letting it emerge after being abandoned and dusty. It will be scary to see yourself emerge from all the filth, but it will also be invigorating because you won't be standing in your way anymore. You will be helping yourself to strive for more and be a greater person. Self-confidence is infectious, so it will spread good energies to the people you love and maybe help them find their true, confident selves as well.

You can face your trauma. It's time to finally unveil the deep hurts that you've tried to push down in your gut. You've tried to escape them so that they don't hurt you, but as they lay dormant inside of you, they are hurting you. They are a thorn in your side that you have not removed in fear that when you remove it you will bleed out. You may bleed a little, but your traumas won't destroy you. You can treat them and recover from years of untreated hurt. Have hope that your wounds will someday fade into barely visible scars. You'll be okay soon.

You can learn who you are. You can take the time right now to learn about yourself. Try new things and explore the world in new ways to figure out who you are. Don't predetermine yourself based on who you'd like to be. Let yourself be discovered organically. Treat yourself with compassion and assure yourself that at the end of the journey, you'll be more aware of yourself and your skills than you have been. You won't have to be afraid anymore. You'll be free to live your life without all the self-doubt that has consumed you and has taken away your personality. Your personality has never gone away. You just need to find where it has been buried.

You can be true to yourself. There's no need to try to please other people at the expense of yourself. There's also no need to pretend to be someone you are not just so you will be accepted. You are who you are, and that person is amazing. You are worth having your own space to be unique and grow. If you aren't true to yourself, you can never love yourself. There will always be troubling levels of shame and doubt. You will avoid doing things that will make you feel fulfilled by pretending to be fulfilled by things that aren't true to you. When you are yourself, you face the risk of being scrutinized and rejected, but it's better to be yourself and mocked than to be accepted as someone else. You deserve to find a place in the world that accepts you as you are.

You can stop letting how other people see you control how you act. It doesn't matter how you were in the past. You are free to be how you please now without relying on what other people think to control how you feel or behave. You are an autonomous person, and only you can define how you identify yourself. You have to find the courage to bravely be yourself even when it is hard because those hard times are when you have the most opportunity to be proud. It is when people tell you that you should be ashamed, and you are not that you feel most confident.

You can embrace everything that you are and feel good about the person you see in the mirror. It's time to accept the person you are because if you don't, your low self-esteem will destroy your attempts at being happy and healthy. The person you can be is hiding under all the fears and insecurities that threaten to suffocate you, but you are resilient. You can fight all the negativity and traumas that make it hard to love yourself. When you address all the things that hurt you, you can start finding ways to help yourself. You can emerge from the steel cocoon of self-doubt and emerge more beautiful and stronger than ever. It's time to stop being afraid of who you are. Love yourself for a change because only when you do will you be confident.

CONCLUSION

You've made it to the end of *Self-Esteem for Beginners*. You now have the tools that you need to begin understanding the roots of your self-esteem issues. You also have the tools that you need to fix those issues and build more confidence. Those of you who struggle with confidence probably know how detrimental low self-esteem can be. You have probably felt it stand between you and what you want to happen. You don't need to let your self-doubt inhibit you anymore. You can work to believe in yourself. You are a worthy person. All you have to do is find ways to cherish that worth.

Your work should not end when you close this book. You need to remain aware of the concepts presented within so that you can embrace who you are and find reasons to believe in yourself. Self-confidence takes work, and it may take weeks, months, or even years to fully build your confidence, but when you start making changes, you will feel different almost immediately. When you are self-confident, all your other issues will become easier to handle, and you'll find yourself thriving in ways that you never even imagined before.

A review on Amazon would be much appreciated if this book was useful for you. Further, spread this book to people in your life who may also need help building their self-esteem and reaching their full potential as confident people! Everyone has a seedling of self-confidence that can be grown to overtake any self-doubt that they have. Anyone can be confident if they commit to themselves.

DESCRIPTION

One of the most troubling issues that people face is low self-esteem. Commonly, people let their doubts, traumas, and insecurities cause them to believe that they are not worthy or that they will never be successful. They feel trapped in their own bodies, and they yearn to be someone else. Someone who feels better, looks better, and is more competent. The secret to self-esteem is that you don't need to change who you are. Rather, you need to learn how to embrace who you are right now. No more running away from yourself. It's time to look in the mirror and to love what you see, both within and without.

Self-Esteem for Beginners is a concise guide to building your self-esteem and finding the vibrant you that is hidden beneath your self-doubt. There is a person in you that is waiting to be free and to succeed. No matter how much success you have now, you can have more success when you put aside your worries and let yourself be freely yourself. This book will liberate you from the self-destructive tendencies that you inevitably have, and it will show you how to turn your weaknesses into strengths. Further, it will highlight stories of real people who have addressed their low self-esteem and have used confidence to turn their lives around.

This book will:
- Show you how to determine if you have self-esteem issues and figure out how they influence your life
- Help you become more aware of the bad habits you have that reduce your self-esteem
- Explain common causes for self-esteem
- Give a detailed explanation of the psychology behind low self-esteem
- Guide you to love yourself and resist the negative sources that convince you that you should hate yourself
- Illustrate how people can rediscover who they are after not being in touch with themselves
- Encourage you to face your fears, fears that drive your self-esteem
- Motivate you to address trauma or other experiences that are the root of your self-esteem problems
- Challenge you to stop caring so much about what other people think
- Ensure that you have all the tools you need to be more confident and can accomplish more in your life
- Free you from the confining binds of self-doubt and self-hate

It is time to put an end to your self-esteem issues because they won't help you get anywhere in life. You don't need to let them impede your well-being anymore. As soon as you start to tackle your low self-esteem, you will see that you will have so many more possibilities to embrace. You will not only feel better about yourself, but you will be able to build stronger relationships with other people that are fueled by love rather than fear. Self-esteem transforms your life in ways that you cannot predict. It makes it easier to do better without having to work harder. Low self-esteem can easily be a thing of your past. Your future will be bright with all the goodness that self-esteem can bring you. Your journey to self-esteem can begin right now!

SELF-CONFIDENCE FOR BEGINNERS

Ultimate Guide to Increase Self-Discipline, Build Self-Confidence, Develop High Self-Esteem, and Realize Your Value

Elizabeth Wright

© Copyright 2020 by Elizabeth Wright. All right reserved.

The work contained herein has been produced with the intent to provide relevant knowledge and information on the topic on the topic described in the title for entertainment purposes only. While the author has gone to every extent to furnish up to date and true information, no claims can be made as to its accuracy or validity as the author has made no claims to be an expert on this topic. Notwithstanding, the reader is asked to do their own research and consult any subject matter experts they deem necessary to ensure the quality and accuracy of the material presented herein.

This statement is legally binding as deemed by the Committee of Publishers Association and the American Bar Association for the territory of the United States. Other jurisdictions may apply their own legal statutes. Any reproduction, transmission or copying of this material contained in this work without the express written consent of the copyright holder shall be deemed as a copyright violation as per the current legislation in force on the date of publishing and subsequent time thereafter. All additional works derived from this material may be claimed by the holder of this copyright.

The data, depictions, events, descriptions and all other information forthwith are considered to be true, fair and accurate unless the work is expressly described as a work of fiction. Regardless of the nature of this work, the Publisher is exempt from any responsibility of actions taken by the reader in conjunction with this work. The Publisher acknowledges that the reader acts of their own accord and releases the author and Publisher of any responsibility for the observance of tips, advice, counsel, strategies and techniques that may be offered in this volume.

INTRODUCTION

Congratulations on purchasing *Self-Confidence for Beginners,* and thank you for doing so.

Walk into any bookstore, and you'll find plenty of books of self-confidence. Browse online, and you'll find thousands of websites talking about self-confidence as they encourage us to be a more confident version of ourselves. You'll find audiobooks, ebooks, podcasts, YouTube videos, and more, all talking about the same subject. The art of self-confidence is talked about everywhere in our society.

Confidence seekers are everywhere. They may not openly talk about it, but most people you pass on the street or even people you know directly could be secretly searching for the key to becoming a more confident person. If you want the very best out of life in every single area of your life, then confidence is the only way to achieve that outcome. When you're confident, you like yourself more. People like you a lot more too. They respect you. They listen to what you have to say. Right now, you're either insecure, or you're confident. There is no in-between, and if you're reading this book, you're probably the first option. But that is okay because confidence is something that can always be fixed. Through this book, you are going to learn to become the confident person that you want to be.

Does being confident mean you're going to be perfect? Or that you're never going to make mistakes ever again. Not at all. You are always going to make mistakes at some point, because like everyone else, that is what we do as humans. We make mistakes. If mistakes didn't exist, how would we ever learn from them? Through this book, you are going to learn the core principles of becoming a more confident person. To attract anything you want in life, you need confidence. You could be the most good looking, talented person in the world, but if you don't have confidence on your side, nobody is going to notice. Why? Because you'll subconsciously always be trying to hide. To fade into the background and stay out of the spotlight.

Confidence can never come from external factors. It has to come from within. Confidence is such a vital aspect of living a successful, happier, and more fulfilled life because, without confidence, you can be sure that the dominant thoughts and emotions you will have are going to be *negative*. It might not be happening 24/7, but every now and then, you're going to feel unhappy, miserable, depressed, and frustrated with yourself and your life in general. If you're always carrying these negative thoughts and emotions with you, it's going to be very difficult for you to accomplish any goal in life. Let's do something to fix that right now.

There are plenty of books on this subject on the market; thanks again for choosing this one! Every effort was made to ensure it is full of as much useful information as possible; please enjoy!

CHAPTER 1
Drop Your Old Mindset - What Self-Confidence Truly Means

Why do we care so much about confidence? Why do we associate this trait with success? Of course, we all want to be successful, and therefore, we believe we need to be more confident to land that job, get that raise, build the business of our dreams, network like a pro, and so on. You might even be wondering if successful people become more confident, or whether confidence is something they gain along the way with every victory and years of experience.

Here's another intriguing question to ponder: *Can confidence be manipulated?* Is it possible to make someone feel more confident at the moment? Can we fake it until we make it? Yes, we can because luckily for us, confidence is a skill that we can build. It is a quality that we can cultivate through deliberate action and changes to your mindset. We're capable of incredible change when we put our minds to it. The person you are today is not the same person you were yesterday, a week ago or a month ago. The version of you today is not going to be the same version of you in the future. That's because you are changed and shaped by the experiences you go through. Change is an inevitable part of life, but the way you change is entirely up to you. You can choose to change for the better, to learn from your experiences, and to use them to improve. Or you can choose to let those experiences hold you back and affect your confidence.

What Is Confidence?

Each one of us has thoughts and feelings. These thoughts and feelings come and go as we go about our day. Confidence is a magnifier of your thoughts. Some people trust their thoughts and use them to their advantage. For example, some people believe they would be brilliant as an entrepreneur, so they do something about it, and they go after that dream of theirs. That's an example of what confidence can do.

Confidence is what separates those who are living happy and fulfilled lives from the ones who feel like their life is going nowhere. If you think about it, a lot of superior achievements throughout history were not solely based on brainpower or incredible talent alone. It was the strange buoyancy of the soul that surged these successful individuals forward. It was *confidence* that had an important role to play, yet it also happens to be a trait that is easily overlooked. This incredible life-changing skill is not something you're going to learn about in your high school textbooks. That would explain why so many people struggle to grasp an understanding of what this concept truly entails. Confidence isn't an innate part of a lot of people. Some people are born with a natural inclination for it, while other people have to work for it.

When you have the courage to accept and embrace your imperfections, that is how you know you're confident and comfortable in your own skin. When you realize that nothing is ever going to be perfect and all you can do is try your best, that's the moment you reach the confidence levels you need to chase after your dreams. Confidence begins with the ability to forgive yourself for the mistakes you make along the way to greatness instead of doing what so many people tend to do. Beat themselves up repeatedly over the mistakes they have made in the past. It is impossible to love yourself or even begin to feel remotely confident when there is an inner voice inside your head that keeps harping on the negative. If the negative things about yourself are the only thing you can focus on, you have very little hope of ever building up any kind of self-confidence.

Why We Lack the Self-Confidence We Need

It goes back thousands of years. Given the life people in the early civilizations lived back then, opportunities were few and far between. So very different from the world that we are living in today. Most of the people would never go beyond their current station or even leave the town they were born in. It became a survival mechanism to keep their heads down and work as a way to avoid the pain of disappointment by expecting and hoping that there was more to life than this. Despite how far we have come, we still carry a little bit of that legacy from the past. We're afraid of disappointment. We don't want to risk being hurt, and that makes hope feel dangerous.

In the world we live in today, we're subtly surrounded by subconscious messages that imply we shouldn't get our hopes too high. It could be in the form of parents or family members, perhaps even friends, colleagues, and other people we may know, who questioned the ideas we talked about. Statements like *"Are you sure you want to do that? That sounds difficult, you might fail if you try"* are examples of the kind of statements that, if exposed to for too long, can slowly chip away at our confidence. Still, we can't blame them entirely. They were merely voicing their concerns, and they did it with good intentions. Even more so when family and close friends are concerned. They say things like that because they don't want to see us fail. They want to protect us from getting hurt. We would probably try and do the same for our loved ones too.

Schools were not the most confidence-inducing experience. Schools rarely encourage you to think outside the box. They want you to be well-behaved, follow the rules, do your homework, study, and get the grades you need to get you into university. The peers we had in school may or may not have helped to either bolster your confidence or bring it crashing down. When you lack confidence, that is when fear becomes bigger than anything else, and it becomes the only thing that matters. It cripples you, paralyzes you because your fear has become so strong it gets to a point where it consumes you, and you become so afraid that you eventually become incapable of doing or reacting to anything.

What We Lack Will Be Our Downfall

Oh yes, a lack of confidence is sure to be your downfall. It invokes nothing but feelings of negativity within you, and it becomes impossible to feel happy or look at the brighter side of life when all you can focus on is how unhappy you feel. When you lack confidence, it becomes easier to see the worst qualities than it is to see the good things you can do. In some extreme cases, poor self-esteem can even lead to feelings of depression and anxiety.

Confidence is something that can be fixed, but first, you need to identify the signs that you might not be as confident as you would like (if you don't already know it):

- **You're Not Assertive Enough** - Struggling to voice your needs is a sign that you lack confidence. You're hesitant about speaking up because you don't want to appear too demanding. You feel awkward about asking for a well-deserved promotion or talking about how you need to feel more supported in your relationship with your significant other. Even though you have every right to voice your concerns and needs, you still hold back because, well, you're not confident enough. Despite knowing that speaking your mind is going to be in your best interest, you're still reluctant to do it. The problem with this approach is that you end up neglecting yourself, and that is never good since it leads to eventual resentment and frustration at the world and yourself. You are the only one who can look after your needs. If you don't do something about it, no one else will. If you don't learn to be confident, you're always going to end up prioritizing someone else's needs above your own. Assertiveness goes hand-in-hand with confidence because it reminds you that you are worthy and deserving. Your needs *matter* just as much as everyone else's.
- **You're Always Explaining Yourself** - Even when you don't need to, you have this need to explain yourself. Sometimes in a long and lengthy way. You always seem to explain your choices, justifying and apologizing if you feel like you might be letting someone down. This makes you an *Explainer*. An *Explainer* is someone who is always waiting for permission and seeking approval from others over the personal choices they want to make. *You don't have to do this;* you know that you don't. But you can't help yourself because, well, you're not confident enough to stand by your choices without feeling guilty. Maybe those explanations are an honest attempt on your part to try and connect to the other person, but it is still an indication that you

lack confidence. The intense desire to be liked and approved of by others is the reason you feel the need to explain yourself. This makes you a *People Pleaser,* and if you don't build the confidence you need, you're always going to be bothered by what someone else thinks about you.

- **You Make Excuses When You Make Mistakes** - Do you catch yourself making excuses immediately after you've messed up? Did you make excuses when something didn't go your way? Confident people do not give excuses for their mistakes. For example, if you were sitting at the table having lunch with a friend and you accidentally bump your water glass, causing the water to spill all over the table, you would immediately say, *"I'm so sorry, I'm so tired today I'm not concentrating properly,"* or *"Sorry about that! The glass was too close to my elbow."* Confident people do not try to explain their mistakes because they know that *everyone* makes mistakes. It happens, and there's nothing wrong with that. You're only human, and you don't need to make excuses whenever you mess up by accident. A confident person would say, *"Sorry about that guys! I'll clean that up,"* and move on. That's confidence.
- **When You're Alone, You Pretend to Be Busy On Your Phone** - You're not busy, but you try to make it look like you are so you don't have to feel awkward about the fact that you're on your own. Do you tend to do this a lot? Especially at social events and when you're out in public by yourself. Sitting alone can feel awkward, but confident people don't mind because they don't worry about what other people think about them. So they're sitting alone, that's okay. Maybe they don't know everyone at the social event, that's okay too. They're perfectly comfortable enjoying their own company or striking up a conversation with someone new. That is what confidence can do for you.
- **Compliments Make You Uncomfortable** - How do you respond when someone offers you a compliment? Do you reply by saying thank you? Or make excuses again like *"No, not really, I'm not that good at it."* When someone offers you a compliment without you having to fish for it, most of the time they mean it. Unless they are trying to butter you up and make you feel good so you will be more inclined to say yes. But most of the time, compliments are sincere, and they are meant to make you feel good about yourself. When someone offers you a nice compliment, and you push back against that by making excuses or downplaying the compliment, that is a clear sign that you lack confidence. Compliments are a struggle for you; even a simple thank you seems difficult.

Is It the Same as Self-Esteem? Not Really

Confidence is often confused with self-esteem. The latter focuses on how much you *like yourself,* the way you feel about yourself, and whether you're happy with the current version of yourself. Confidence, on the other hand, is about how *self-assured* you are. Confidence and self-esteem are *not* the same things. You could be highly confident or doubtful in both a good or a bad assessment of yourself. Confidence and self-esteem may not be similar, but there is one thing they share in common. They are both counter-productive traits that will lead to inaction because you simply feel too awkward, shy, reluctant, and worse, you don't believe that you can achieve success. Therefore, you will let a lot of opportunities slip through your fingers, some opportunities which could have changed your life in a tremendous way because you didn't have enough courage to grab onto them and hold on tight with both hands. Without confidence or self-esteem, you never know what you could be missing out on, whether it is a potential chance to network for the betterment of your career, forge new friendships and even build important connections.

If you think you're afraid to fail, think about this: *A lack of confidence and self-esteem is going to lead to the one thing that you should be afraid of. Never attempting to go after what you want. That is what you should be afraid of.* Imagine if some of the people who have left legacies that last a lifetime was too afraid to try. What if Thomas Edison had been afraid to keep going because he failed a thousand times at making the lightbulb. We would have been forced to live in darkness for a longer period. Imagine if the Wright Brothers were afraid to build their first airplane because they were afraid they might fail and come crashing down. We might never have had the chance to travel the world in the plane if no one else besides the Wright Brothers thought about this idea. Many of the inventions and modern-day conveniences we enjoy today would not exist if their creators were afraid to go for what they wanted. The possibility of failure is always going to be there. But having the courage and confidence to go ahead and do it anyway despite the possibility of failure, that is the quality that makes self-confidence so remarkably life-changing.

Can You Really *Feel* More Confident Just By Thinking Positive Thoughts?

Well, that depends on how you *feel* when you're thinking these positive thoughts. For example, think about this sentence: *I am intelligent, and I am attractive.* While you're saying it, nod your head up and down, agree with that statement. How does that make you feel? Say it a few times until it starts to sound natural. Now, think about that same sentence again, but this time, shake your head left and right. Disagree with the statement you're thinking about. How does it make you feel? Here is another example: *I am a strong, intelligent, confident person.* When you're thinking this statement, stand up tall, throw your shoulders back, puff your chest forward, and adopt the superman pose. Say this statement repeatedly and smile when you do. How does it make you feel? Now, say the same statement, but this time slump your shoulders and hunch over, looking down like you're afraid to make eye contact. How does that make you feel?

That's the magnification effect. When you think positive thoughts and then exude the actions that back those thoughts up, your confidence levels seem to magnify. This is how those who have achieved success have been using their positive thoughts to power them along. The answer, therefore, is *yes*. You *can* make yourself feel more confident and fake it until you make it by using the appropriate actions to back up your positive, self-empowering thoughts. One of the biggest stumbling blocks in our lives is the tendency for our minds to hold onto negative thoughts. A negative mindset is easier to fall into because it requires a lot less work. Cultivating a mindset that focuses so hard on the positivity that nothing will sway it is the one that requires a lot of hard work.

But overcoming this stumbling block is the very first step you need to start building the confidence you've always hoped for. Understandably, being negative seems to come a lot easier, but if you want to start building that confident personality for yourself instead of just admiring it on others, you're going to have to change your mind, and this means slowly getting rid of negativity. Successful people always preach about one core concept, and that concept is cultivating a positive mind. To learn how to see the silver lining in the situations that you have to go through. Evaluate the people who are the closest to you, are they a positive influence, or are they negative influence. Keeping a close circle of positive people is essential to making this technique effective. This must be one of your core priorities from this point forward. To be positive, even if you don't feel like doing it, do it. Do it until it becomes second nature to you. Napoleon Hill once said if you can see it in your mind and believe in it, then you can achieve it. Visualization is such a powerful tool that, unfortunately, very often gets underestimated the same way confidence does. But did you ever stop to think that if you can visualize all the bad scenarios and things that could go wrong and believe in it so much that it manifests itself physically and is strong enough to stop you from doing something, why can't it work the other way around? If you can visualize the negative, then you can visualize the positive, and if you want to start building up the confidence to be able to small talk with any stranger, you're going to have to start focusing more on the positive visualization aspect.

You need to visualize the life that you want for yourself. You need to visualize that you're confident, happy, successful. That you're just as good as everyone else out there, and you deserve to chase after your goals the same way they did. Nothing is a bigger confidence killer than thinking someone is better than you are and wishing you were more like them. This is a common pattern that can be seen in those who suffer from low self-esteem, which is why they tend to shy away from others and beat themselves up all the time by constantly thinking they're never good enough or never going to be as good enough as someone else. *Visualize, visualize, visualize.* Spend every free moment you have pictured yourself as a confident person, a person who is interesting, and a person people want to talk to whenever you're in a room or a gathering. Picture yourself thriving in every conversation, and cement that image strongly in your mind until it starts to manifest itself into reality. Don't forget about the accompanying actions like nodding your head and standing up tall with a smile on your face to back up this mental image.

Confidence Is More Than a Need. It's A Necessity.
Being confident will shift your perspective on a lot of things, including how you view talking to people and the relationships that you form with them. When you're confident, there is no room for negativity in your life anymore, especially as your belief in yourself grows stronger over time. People naturally gravitate towards people who exude positivity and have a great outlook on life, and that will, in turn, make handling small talk sessions a much easier process for you. Confidence begins in your mind, and it is a state of mind that you and only you have the power to change. You must want to change the way you think about yourself and let go of all those negative connotations you previously associated with yourself. There are plenty of ways you can help to strengthen your mindset over time to tell yourself that you are a confident person who is more than capable of handling anything that comes your way.

Confidence is considered a soft skill, and you need both hard and soft skills in life to succeed. Once you embrace the idea that you *need* to have confidence in your life, you can begin taking the necessary steps to start building the confident mindset needed to help you get anything you want in life. Yes, you need to embrace the idea of confidence is a necessity first because this is the only way to open your mind and be receptive to the steps that must be taken. If you don't, you're going to subconsciously resist these steps, and everything is either going to feel difficult or unnatural. Open your mind to the idea that if you want to succeed, this is what you need. A shift in your mindset is the first step in the process. You need to start perceiving yourself and the world around you differently. Confidence is built through practice and relevant experience. What does relevant experience mean? It is simply building the experience that you need in the area that you want to improve your confidence in. For example, giving a speech for the 10th time is going to be a lot less nerve-wracking compared to your first time. William Jennings Bryan, the former U.S Secretary of State, once said: *"The way to develop self-confidence is to do the thing you fear and get a record of successful experience behind you."* Basically, you need to practice standing up to what makes you nervous and uncomfortable.

It is time to create a shift in your mindset and be proud of everything you are. Be proud of your strengths and embrace your weaknesses. They both define the person that you are. A positive state of mind will always win out at the end of the day. It may require a lot more work since negativity has a stronger influence, but it always wins. Always. Even the most confident people today have to fight hard to keep negativity at bay, and that includes developing the ability to separate themselves from their weaknesses. Once you have built that foundation of strengths to focus on, it's time to identify what your weak spots are. There will be some qualities you might never be able to change, and it's okay to accept those flaws. Nobody out there is perfect, and you shouldn't put that pressure on yourself to be flawless either. Greater strength comes from the ability to accept both your flaws and your weaknesses, and once you've identified the weak spots you can improve on, focus on ways to make them better. Our brains are naturally wired for negativity, and it takes the brain four times longer to store good things than bad. We search for flaws before we focus on strengths, and we prefer to criticize before we complement them. We're instinctively drawn to negativity, and we don't treat ourselves any differently. Your confidence lies in your ability to pay attention to your talents, your strengths, your achievements, and the advantages you have to offer. Commit time each day to remind yourself of your strengths to start boosting your confidence.

What Confident People *Don't Do*

Confidence is not the same as egotistical swagger. When people believe in themselves and their abilities, they don't need to be boastful or arrogant. Confident people display certain behaviors that set them apart from everyone else, and here are some behaviors they definitely *don't* engage in:

- **They Don't Focus Too Much on Appearances** - Confident people accept themselves for the way they are. They love their bodies and the way they look, size, flaws, and all. They look after their bodies and eat healthy food because they know they deserve to be well looked after.
- **They Don't Try to Change Who They Are** - You will never catch a truly confident person trying to be someone that they are not. It doesn't matter if they are an introvert or extrovert. Confidence comes from within, and both personality types are capable of exuding confidence. They know that feeling good about who they are leads to self-assurance. They know they can achieve so much more if they stay authentic and remain true to who they are. They learned long ago that self-acceptance is a vital part of

becoming a confident person, that is why you'll never see them trying to be someone else or being fake just to fit in.

- **They Don't Compare** - Put a stop to the comparison, and you'll find that you're much happier when you do. There is no point in comparing yourself to someone else because the truth is, you're never going to be that person. You're as unique as your thumbprint is. No two people are alike; the same way no two sets of thumbprints will ever be alike. It's how we distinguish ourselves from the rest. Comparison is a destructive habit, and it will do nothing to help the successful mindset you're trying to build. You're unique, and you have the potential to reach your own kind of success. To become more confident, that pernicious voice in your mind must be silenced.

- **They Don't Crave Likes and Follows on Social Media** - If someone likes something they've shared, great! If they don't, that's okay too. A confident person is not bothered by superficial likes and follows on social media. Confident people don't need social media to feel good about themselves. They don't need social media to validate that they are awesome. To the confident person, social media is merely an entertaining place to share content and maybe catch up with what other people are doing. Their profiles are usually filled with interesting content since they tend to be less self-centered than those who are on social media fishing for compliments.

- **They Don't Think Other People Know Best** - They never assume that other people always know better than they do. Confident people trust their own judgment and never look to others for validation or approval. They value their opinions and listen to their own intuition. They trust that they know what is in their best interest, and they are confident enough to carry out actions even if others disagree with them. They may seek guidance or input from trusted sources, but they end up making the final decision when the time comes.

- **They Don't Wait for Anyone's Permission** - A confident person will never need someone else to tell them what to do all the time. The only time the confident person asks a lot of questions or looks to others is when they are new at something or trying to familiarize themselves with a routine or a new situation. They rarely ever wait to be told what to do. They see what needs to be done, and they are confident enough in their abilities to get the job done.

- **They Never Put Someone Else Down** - Confident people don't feel the need to put other people down to make themselves feel good. They're not afraid of competition. In fact, they welcome it and use the competition as motivation to do even better. They don't feel the need to undermine others, and this is something you'll never find them doing. If they do notice that certain toxic people around them are indulging in this kind of behavior, they move away from that. When someone else succeeds, they are genuinely happy for those people. Rather than resent someone else's success, the confident person uses that as motivation for themselves to do better.

- **They Don't Try to Dominate Conversations** - Confident people treat conversations like an exchange of healthy ideas and thoughts. They don't try to dominate a conversation just to prove they are more interesting, or that they know better. They don't mind doing the listening if it means they get to learn a little bit about what someone else is passionate about.
- **They Don't Actively Try and Avoid Conflict** - Confident people understand that conflict is a part of life. You're not always going to get along with everyone around you. Once in a while, heads will butt, and they are confident enough to stand up for themselves if they feel the need to. For the confident person, conflict is something that can be managed effectively, and thus, they don't try to run away from it, live in denial, or try to people-please their way through life in the hopes of avoiding conflict.
- **They Don't Cling to Others** - You'll never find a confident person who is needy and desperate. It goes with the territory of being comfortable enough in their own skin that they don't fear being alone sometimes. They do enjoy the company of others, but at the same time, they're comfortable enough to enjoy their own company.
- **They Don't Depend on External Elements for Happiness** - They don't rely on social media for happiness. They don't depend on the approval and acceptance of others for happiness. Happiness is a very *critical* element of confidence. To be happy with what you do, you need to be happy with who you are. Those who are brimming with confidence derive pleasure from the sense of satisfaction they get from a job well done. They know happiness comes from within, and no matter what anyone else may think, they understand you are never as good or bad as people say you are. That is true confidence.

CHAPTER 2
Moving Out Of Your Comfort Zone

Would you believe it if you were told that the more you subjected yourself to discomfort, the *happier* you will be? Think about all those times you had to step out of your comfort zone. Yes, it was uncomfortable. Yes, you felt like quitting and giving up. You might have even questioned several times, *"Why am I doing this?."* The problem is, not everyone is willing to regularly push themselves to step out of their comfort zones. Especially if you lack confidence in yourself and your abilities.

What Is a Comfort Zone?

A comfort zone is actually a psychological state of mind. It happens when you're comfortable and familiar with your surroundings and your routine. You will know you're in your comfort zone when you feel at ease, and you feel like you are in control of your environment. In their comfort zones, most people experience lower levels of stress and anxiety because, well, they have some sense of control over themselves and their current environment. Is it possible to still perform when you're in your comfort zone? Yes, it is, but your performance is only going to be steady or stagnated. That is because you're working at a certain pace that you're already comfortable and familiar with, which means you're probably not pushing yourself harder the way you could be.

Author Judith M. Bardwick explains in her book, *The Dangers Of the Comfort Zone,* that this zone is typically where a person can operate from an anxiety-neutral position. University of Houston Graduate College of Social Work research professor, Brene Brown, describes the comfort zone as a place where vulnerability, uncertainty, and scarcity are at minimal levels. When we feel we have some semblance of control, we're content and comfortable. Hence the term comfort zone.

The idea of stepping *outside* of these zones and into uncertainty where we can't control what might happen causes anxiety for many people. If we're already comfortable in a certain way, why bother trying to change that? The problem with getting too comfortable in your comfort zone is, you end up not wanting to get out of that zone. Why would you when it's just so comfortable? A lack of confidence would just aggravate the situation even more, because when we become too complacent with the way things are, subconsciously we start to seek out reasons and excuses to avoid any kind of responsibility that would push us out of that comfort zone. We love to do what we're comfortable with, and this is why we find it so hard to venture outside our comfort zone. We love familiarity, and we're resistant to change because it makes it uncomfortable. Comfort zones keep you safe from the possibility of failure, judgment, criticism, stress, and all those unpleasant feelings you have to go through before you reach the peak of your success. These are all valid concerns too. No wonder it is such a struggle to decide to leave this zone. Even more so when you're not confident that you can achieve a successful outcome if you do make that choice.

But This Is a Dangerous Zone to Be In

We don't want to admit it, but we love what is familiar and comfortable. Going back to old habits and familiar patterns seem like a better option instead of having to deal with the unknown. An unknown where there is a real possibility you might fail or risk not being good enough. Change creates a new awareness, new perspective, poses a huge threat to what has been so comfortable and familiar. Even if what was once so comfortable and familiar is no longer satisfying or fulfilling. No matter which way you turn, you're faced with the prospect of destroying what you have just learned you want or destroying who you have been now that you've learned you want to become someone new. As if that wasn't bad enough, with all the stress coming from the prospect of change, you've now ignited the stress response in your body that creates a cascade of stress-related illnesses or symptoms. It becomes so much easier to self-sabotage than you have to deal with all this pressure. It becomes so much easier to decide to stay in your comfort zone.

Comfort zones keep you stuck where you are, but at the same time, they keep you safe. Your head is spinning with all sorts of questions about how change is going to impact your life, what relationships might be lost along the way, what you would need to sacrifice. It all becomes too much to deal with at some point. Some people are so resistant to change, and they're terrified of it to the point where they self-sabotage. We self-sabotage because we don't like it when something is too risky or uncertain. If given the choice, we would all prefer to stay in our comfort zones. Self-sabotage is what happens when you're approaching the edge of that comfort zone or when you've passed that comfort zone line.

What makes the comfort zone so dangerous is that your mind starts to convince you that the struggle is not worth it, and you start doing things that don't allow you to overcome the challenges you face. The changes you know you'll have to face could create such a snowball domino effect. You begin to do anything you can to protect yourself from feeling that kind of anxiety. Success is hard work. Overcoming challenges is hard work. Change to achieve success is great, but at the same time, it could impact so much you're afraid of what is to come. There's a mental or subconscious part of you that tells you to backtrack or give up when something becomes too hard. Having to evict the zone that you feel comfortable in is not an easy pill to swallow. You will be tested, pushed to your limits; at times, you may cry and feel like you want to give up. It's hard to see it when it is happening, but every challenge that you face from the moment you leave your comfort zone is making you stronger. Every challenge is designed to make you a better person if you can see it through to the end.

No matter how good that zone may feel, what makes you comfortable is going to ruin you. You *need* to encounter hardship to grow as a person. Only in a state of discomfort can we continue to grow. The environment that you live in is going to dictate whether you grow or remain stuck where you are. Your environment is going to either promote your growth or hinder it. Think of a goldfish that lives in a fishbowl. The environment that the goldfish lives in will dictate its size. In a fishbowl, it is safe, but it usually doesn't grow very big because the size of the fishbowl is hindering its growth. If that goldfish was placed in a bigger and wider environment, like a pond, for example, there's more room for growth. However, it also faces the danger of being eaten by bigger fish in that environment, so the goldfish has a reason to grow bigger in size to give itself a fighting chance. Your environment is like that proverbial fishbowl. Stay in your comfort zone, and like the goldfish, there is only so much you can grow. But broadening your horizons and the risks that you face will be a motivating factor for you to become stronger than ever to give yourself a fighting chance.

Think of your current environments where you live, work, and play. All of these are proverbial fish bowls that are dictating your current growth. When you live in a state of stagnation in your comfort zone, your creativity and independent thought are stifled. This is why you don't grow much in this zone, and your performance can only go so far. Comfort zones are low-performing growth zones. You need to train your mind to believe you have what it takes to succeed. You might believe that you have a desire to succeed in a certain path, but subconsciously in the back of your mind, you don't believe that you have what it takes to make it happen. If you don't believe you deserve it, you're always going to self-sabotage, even when you think you're not doing it. Life begins when you burst through your comfort zone, and the only way to do that is to get rid of all those self-sabotaging habits that have been holding you back all along. Pushing beyond your comfort zone is like a muscle you work during exercise. It's hard at first, but the more you do it, the easier it starts to become. If you've ever procrastinated, made excuses, lacked clarity suddenly, and even doubt your own greatness, then you need to pay attention.

We Know We Need to Change, So Why Are We Still Hesitating?

Because of the chaos, you're afraid to confront. When you don't have control over what happens around you, it feels like your world is descending into chaos. When your environment is not in order, it is not desirable. When there is no predictability, we become afraid. We're afraid when the outcome is not guaranteed, and we're afraid of what is going to happen to us should we fall flat on our faces. We know being comfortable is dangerous because it means we're not growing as a person. Yet, it feels like a struggle to put one foot in front of the other, pushing yourself out of your comfort zone anyway because, well, we're afraid. *Growth can only happen in a state of discomfort.* Let this be the mantra that pushes you forward.

Yes, you may not feel very confident right now, but there is going to be *zero* chance that you are ever going to become the confident person you hope to be if you continue to stay in your comfort zone. Confidence cannot be developed if you're not moving anywhere. If we think about it, it is not the challenges that we are afraid of most of the time. It is the *unpredictability* and the lack of control that those challenges bring. Not having an outcome that is certain or expected can lead to a lot of "what if" questions. Those questions terrify us because the answers and speculations we make only feed into any existing negative thoughts we might have.

Actively seeking discomfort to become a better, stronger, and more confident person might not be something you want to hear. But it is something you *must-do* if you hope to change for the better. Outside your comfort zone is the only real place that success can be achieved. It is the only place where a greater sense of self-confidence and self-esteem can be developed. Beyond the walls of your comfort zone lie a whole realm of possibilities. The opportunities out there are yours for the taking. But all of this and more cannot happen if you continue to allow yourself to remain *stuck*.

Stepping Out of Your Comfort Zone Can Be a Good Thing
When we have to venture into the unfamiliar, our stress response is triggered. This can be a good thing since it also enhances our level of focus on concentration since our brain is telling us we need to be alert. Believe it or not, your performance can actually be *enhanced* when there's a certain amount of stress introduced into the mix. As uncomfortable as change might be, it's important to consistently remind yourself that change can be a good thing if you let it. Stress is the way our bodies react to the stimuli that it is exposed to. Generally, stress is experienced as a short-term reaction, and it usually goes away, and our bodies return to normal once the cause of the stress has passed. Depending on the way you handle it and how it affects you, stress can either be a good thing or a bad thing. Good stress kicks in to help you pull those long all-nighters to meet important deadlines and push past your boundaries to see what you're capable of. Bad stress, however, leaves you with insomnia, a lack of clarity, and the constant feeling of being on edge like your last nerve is about to snap at any minute.

Sometimes, we voluntarily choose to step out of our comfort zones. Other times, we may be forced into it. Like when our employer suddenly has to let us go because of an economic downturn. When you're forced to leave your comfort zone with no other choice, the way you respond will dictate how much you grow and how much confidence you develop along the way. Other times, we may be encouraged out of our comfort zones by other people who push us to be better. That is one form of good stress. Good stress is the adrenaline rush you need to help you overcome the challenges you face so you can cross the finish line of every goal you set for yourself. Small amounts of good stress keep us challenged, motivated, interested, and continuously striving to do better. To be better. Chaos is good for development. Comfort zones stifle your development.

Breaking Out of Your Comfort Zone Killers

What needs to happen now is that our minds must be retrained. We need to rewire our minds to relish in discomfort. How? By reminding ourselves that these discomforts never last. Like a storm, it comes, and it goes. All we need to do is be strong enough to weather that storm. Before you begin working on building your confidence, the skill that you need to develop first is the skill that helps you break out of your comfort zone. Let's talk about some of the common comfort zone killers and how you can break out of them:

- **You're Letting Fear Keep You In the Zone** - Fear is the biggest comfort zone killer. When we're afraid to face our fears, we tend to rationalize and find reasons *not* to do something. The only way to break out of this comfort zone killer is to acknowledge your fear, but then push yourself to do it anyway. Face up to your fears, no matter how terrified it makes you. Do it one step at the time, put one foot in front of the other. You don't have to dive headfirst of the deep end when you're afraid. It is okay to take your time as long as you keep moving forward. What we need to realize is that there is no running away from our fears. Even though it is the easier thing to do, you cannot spend the rest of your life running away from your obstacles. You've only got one short, precious life to live, and if you waste it all by running all the time, you're going to reach your retirement years and look back filled with regret. The most persistent people are the ones more likely to achieve success because they have the discipline and the drive to never give up and always keep moving forward. This is because they are engaged in habits that work for them, and they have diligently trained themselves to have the discipline to stick to these habits. If you want to stop self-sabotage, you need to be persistent and to stop running away from the things that you're afraid of. The self-sabotaging thought will come creeping into your mind, enticing you to give up each time you struggle, but you need to train your mind to be stronger than the thoughts that you have. What we need to realize is that the longer we hesitate and rationalize why we shouldn't do something, the harder it is going to be to face up to your fears. You have to steel yourself and push back against it by doing the hard thing and keep moving forward. Like ripping off a bandaid, do it in one swift, quick motion. No matter what you feel like or what your mind is telling you to do, keep pushing forward.

- **Not Being Focused Enough On Your Goals -** Another comfort zone killer that stops us from moving forward. When you're not focused enough on your goals, you become easily distracted. When you're easily distracted, you lose focus. When you lose focus, it's easy to talk yourself out of not doing something, and the excuses come pouring in. You need to identify what your current behavior patterns are that prevent you from staying focused on your goals. Next, think about what you can do to rectify those patterns. What you need to do is reflect on your daily behavior. Think about this for a minute. Where are you guilty of slowing down when you know you should be speeding up? Reflect on some of the things you've done in the past too. What you're trying to identify are the ways that you've self-sabotaged in the past. What lies outside your comfort zone may feel weird, but you need to remember that challenge only means you're doing something to better yourself. Positive change cannot take place if you choose to stay where you are and never move. Identify when you're feeling resistant when you've pushed a little outside your comfort zone, and then think about what you can do to help you overcome that resistance.
- **Be Willing to Try Something New -** The idea of something new can be both scary and exciting at the same time. It depends entirely on how you choose to look at it. You see, most of the time, we are not willing to try something new because of the limiting beliefs we carry with us. We *think* we're not good enough, not talented enough, not passionate enough, not equipped enough, and we could come up with a whole bunch of other reasons why. But we will never know what the outcome really is unless we *try*. Toss out the limiting beliefs that are holding you back because these only keep you in your comfort zone. If you're afraid of starting your own business, ask yourself why? What's the reason behind that fear? What is that self-limiting belief that is holding you back, and is it justified? Why are you afraid of getting into a serious relationship? What limiting beliefs are holding you back from the belief that the relationship can be happy and fulfilling? Reframe your mindset because you need to believe that you're worthy; otherwise, no matter how hard you work, you're always going to find some obstacle or other blocking you. Part of your new mindset for success needs to be a new belief. A belief that you

deserve all that you desire. Believe that you have what it takes to make your dreams come true. Without the confidence and belief in your own self-worth, you will always find it a challenge to value yourself, love yourself, or even name any positive traits that you may have. You don't have to lose something immediately to get started breaking out of your comfort zone. All you have to do is adopt a willing attitude to try and be open to seeing how it plays out.

- **You're Striving for Perfection** - How often have you told yourself you would be willing to do something *"if only"* it was a certain way. That you would have been willing to do something if *X* or *Y* had been in your favor. Striving for perfectionism is striving for a concept that does not exist. You can never be 100% perfect because no one can. Life simply does not work that way, and we're only human, this means that yes, we do make mistakes from time to time. Holding on to this comfort zone killer is only going to keep you trapped, never moving forward because you're striving for something that does not exist. Novelist and writer Anne Lamott eloquently put it when she said: *Perfectionism is the voice of the oppressor, and it is the enemy of people.* Perfectionism is not all bad, but if you're an over-thinker, this is one habit you need to rid yourself of because of the constant pressure you face to meet unrealistic standards. If you want to break out of your comfort zone, let go of this concept that you need things to be a certain, perfect way before you can move forward. Overthinkers are guilty of using this as an excuse not to budge from their comfort zone. They don't trust their judgment, and they are not confident in their abilities. One part of that is because they struggle with perfectionism that is unrealistic. When they fall short, they feel incompetent and lose confidence in their abilities. Self- doubt can be a crippling burden to bear, and as soon it gets a foothold in your mind, it can be a very tough habit to break out of. We know that we shouldn't focus on the negative. We know we should believe in ourselves. *Perfectionism does not exist*. You worry so much about everything that could go wrong, and you try to overcompensate by attempting to control nearly everything around them to the point of perfectionism. While perfectionism may sound like a good thing, it isn't because it is simply not possible to be perfect all the time. When you fail to gain the control you want, it only makes the negative the limiting beliefs you're telling yourself seem much worse. Let go of perfectionism and instead, just try your best at everything you do.

The Fundamental Steps to Start With
Everybody is afraid of something. Even successful people are afraid of something. We're all afraid of something, and this knowledge can liberate you from putting so much pressure on yourself to be perfect all the time. It can free you from the pressure of thinking you need to be a "certain way" before you can begin taking the steps you need to improve yourself. Your journey to greater confidence begins at the end of your comfort zone. It takes *courage* to do the things that you are afraid of, and this is what you're going to take away from this chapter. The courage to break free of your limiting beliefs. The courage to face the fear of the unknown and what you cannot control. When courage is combined with confidence, you become *unstoppable*. Before you can get to confidence, though, you're going to need to take steps to break out of your comfort zone.

As Winston Churchill once said: *"Courage is rightly considered the foremost of all virtues, for, upon it, all others depend."* The braver you become with each fear you overcome, the more confident you subsequently become too. Don't become one of those people who are so afraid to dream big that they shut themselves down even before they have had a chance to get started. NO, you need to believe that anything is possible if you want it badly enough. To break out of this very limiting bubble of comfort you're living in, this is what you need to do:

- **Commit Wholeheartedly** - It doesn't matter what you're thinking about doing. Commit to it wholeheartedly. Focus entirely on doing it and finishing it. Everything else is secondary. The possibilities of what might happen and the speculations you make are secondary. All successful people achieve victory because they are fully committed and engaged in the task they decide to take on. The phrase "throw yourself entirely into your work" is how you stay focused. Committing completely and wholeheartedly is how you stop yourself from being sidetracked by your fears. Our minds can be resistant to change when it's taking us out of our comfort zone. Life is not always going to go according to plan, and the more willing and prepared you are to adapt and change to the circumstances, the easier it will be for your brain to switch back into the focus mode it needs. It's okay if you don't have a guarantee. All you need to do to overcome your current challenge is to be involved wholeheartedly in your activities. If you fail, at least you know you failed while you were trying your best, and there is always next time to try again. Remember, it took Edison 1,000 tries before he found the lightbulb. If he can try 1,000 times without ever giving up, you can do it too.
- **Have the Courage to Move Into the Discomfort Zone** - The zone where awkwardness and discomfort sometimes rule the

day. The zone where fear and anxieties lead the charge because our fears allow them to be set free. In your quest for success, there is no enemy greater than that of your comfort zone, and the only way to overcome this is to be willing to move into the other zone. The zone that nobody wants to find themselves in. The *discomfort zone*. The thing we need to remember is that the life of our dreams doesn't happen when we're stuck in a rut. It happens when we have the courage we need to relocate. Having the courage to move with only faith on your side and no guarantee of success seems like a lot to ask.

- **Repeatedly Do What You're Afraid Of -** One way of working through your fears is to face it repeatedly until you no longer feel afraid. As you begin preparing to breach your comfort zone boundaries, pick one fear to work on, and focus on overcoming that fear first before you move onto the next fear. For example, if you're afraid of public speaking and giving speeches because you're not feeling confident on stage yet, the only way to get through it is to repeatedly force yourself to give speeches until you're no longer afraid of the stage and the audience anymore. It could take you 10 speeches before you reach this level. Maybe even 20 speeches. But the one thing you will notice is that the minute the fear is gone, it is replaced by confidence. This confidence is only going to grow with each speech you make. Once you feel you have overcome this fear and you're not afraid anymore. It might go against your natural instinct, but you need to start running towards the things you fear. Not away from it. Dominate your fears, and you will feel like a superhero. Try it.

- **Become Your Own Validation -** You don't need anyone else to validate that you're good enough or capable enough. The only validation you need is from yourself because you are the one going through your challenges. No one else is. They will be there as support systems, but this is your solo journey to take. If you base your self-worth on whether other people approve of you or like you, you're going to struggle to break out of your comfort zone forever. If your confidence is based purely on external forces, it's not a firm foothold for you to stand on. The best way to start building your internal validation is to focus and build upon what makes you feel good. When you feel good, then you don't need others to make you feel good. Do activities that make you feel happy, surround yourself with people who make you feel awesome without having to do any favors for them. Focus on your strengths and all your best qualities and block out everything else. You already have a lot going for you; you just need to be reminded of it.

- **Stay Focused on Solutions -** Instead of focusing on how afraid you are, how anxious you feel, or how everything is going to possibly go wrong, stay focused on solutions instead. Stay focused on the solution and block out all other distractions. At every step of the way during your thought process, ask if this is leading you towards a solution. If it's not, then change your train of thought, so you're always focused on finding a solution. The choice is yours to make, and you can choose to ask, *"What do I do from here? What is the next step? How do I overcome this? What options do I have?."* The choice always resides with you, and this is where you have the power. If you're someone who needs to have some sense of control in your life, this is where you can direct your focus towards. You are in control of the solutions you choose to go with.

The final thing you can do to build your confidence and hold onto this confidence when you're breaking out of your comfort zone is to have the courage to persist longer than anyone else. Persistence is one of the few qualities that will ultimately guarantee you succeed as what you're trying to do. When everyone else gives up and quits, you keep going. That is what confidence can do for you, and the more you practice the steps in this chapter, your confidence is only going to grow from this point onwards. You have nothing to fear and everything to gain if you learn to view every failure as a learning experience.

CHAPTER 3
Dealing With Nervous Anxiety

Sweaty palms. Heart palpitations. Nervous nail-biting. Nervous pacing back and forth. These are all indicators that you might be an anxious person. You're probably already familiar with these symptoms, especially when you're faced with the prospect of being in a social situation. When you're anxious, confidence seems like an elusive concept, depending on the severity of your condition. Anxiety can range from mild to nervous. Our bodies have a strange way of reacting when we're anxious, but the one thing that you can be sure of is that you will not be acting in a confident manner.

The problem with anxiety is that it is not a rational thing. We can't just "get over it" and "be confident," even though that is the advice most people would tell you since they don't fully understand what anxiety entails. To them, the solution is simple. Just push aside your fears, snap out of it, and be confident. Easy, right? *Not if you're an anxious person.* It's hard to remain calm, let alone think about being confident when you're fraught with nervousness. Those "you-can-do-it!" motivation type blogs and articles don't seem to help either. Those articles are trying to make you feel good about yourself again, but they're not helping because they lack any actionable or practical advice on how to tackle the root of the problem you're facing, which is your nervous anxiety. The mind can be a very powerful thing, and when it's anxious, it seems to be even more powerful than ever. Trying to put it on pause for even two seconds can require monumental effort and concentration, none of which you have when your mind and heart seems to be racing a mile a minute.

Understanding Anxiety

Originally, anxiety is a survival mechanism present in all of us. Its primary function is to alert us to the presence of danger, and it is not meant to be an emotion that lingers for long. Once the danger has passed, anxiety should dissipate, but that's not the case if you happen to be dealing with an anxiety disorder. With an anxiety disorder, the body remains in an unnatural heightened state of alertness. Everything feels like a cause for alarm, and it triggers a constant flow of cortisol throughout the body. There's no exact reason why you might be feeling nervous or anxious, either. Anxiety has no logical source, making it difficult to pinpoint what the underlying cause may be. It can be difficult to talk yourself out of an anxious episode.

Anxiety is diagnosed as a psychiatric or mental health disorder that is capable of derailing your daily life because of the persistent fear and worry that seems to follow you everywhere you go. In today's society, it is unfortunate that anxiety is not talked about enough the way it should be. This is partly due to the stigma associated with it because it is classified as a mental health issue. It is not uncommon for those struggling with anxiety to be misunderstood, even by those who are closest to them. Anxiety can be a very lonely and isolating burden to bear when you feel disconnected to the people closest to you. A lot of people who struggle with anxiety are often embarrassed to admit what they're going through because they fear being rejected.

It's hard to describe what anxiety feels like, but the closest description would be anxiety makes you feel like you're running in a hamster wheel, going round and round in circles with no productive solution or end in sight. Your days and nights seem to be filled with persistent worries that won't seem to go away, no matter how hard the person may try to reason with themselves. The fear felt can sometimes be so great that it leads to a panic attack episode. There seems to be a persistent sense of foreboding or dread like something bad is going to happen at any time. When you're anxious, your body remains in an unnatural heightened state of alertness. Everything feels like a cause for alarm, and it triggers a constant flow of cortisol throughout the body. No wonder you find it such a struggle to remain confident. It's not an easy thing to do when you've got a lot going on.

What Happens to Our Bodies When We're Anxious

Ice cold hands and feet is one symptom of extreme anxiety. That is because when you're anxious, your blood flow is all channeled toward your larger organs. This makes it hard for your blood to circulate properly throughout your body, and that is why you could look pale and feel ice-cold even when it's hot outside. Your body is going into its fight or flight mode to help you survive. When you're anxious, you could also be prone to eating and drinking more quickly, which could lead to excessive gas in your body. You might find that you need to go to the toilet a lot more frequently too because the muscles tensing up in your body are going to put some pressure on some of your internal organs. Like your bladder, for example. Muscle tension is a common side effect of nervous anxiety.

Anxious individuals, like those with Generalized Anxiety Disorder, find that they tend to breathe more rapidly than other people do. When you breathe rapidly, your brain is tricked into thinking that you need more oxygen. This will cause you to take deep breaths, and sometimes, you end up yawning a lot to try and get more oxygen flow to the brain. Have you got an uncomfortable itch? Anxiety could be behind that too. Because you're anxious, it could make you more prone to a lot of skin allergies and problems like developing a rash when you're extremely stressed. That's the extra cortisol churning through your body. When all those hormones are rushing through your veins, your skin starts to feel irritated.

Do you find that you have difficulty concentrating? Well, that could be because of your anxiety too. Sometimes it feels like you're having an out of body experience, especially when things start to feel too overwhelming. Everything starts to feel surreal, and there is a reason for this. It is because your body is going through what is known as the fight or flight response. Oh, and frequent headaches and migraines could also be a potential side effect of this condition. The tension and the pressure brought on by staying in a period of prolonged negativity is like putting a tight rubber band around your head, constricting it. This can cause a lot of pressure and discomfort, and you might feel like your head is about to explode at times when you're so overwhelmed by your thoughts. Headaches and migraines are a common symptom among those who struggle with excessive thoughts that also happen to trigger their anxiety.

When you're stressed out all the time, you're not a confident person. Instead, what you become is an irritable, impatient, and sometimes angry person. Being in a stressed-out state all the time will leave anyone feeling on edge, and this happens a lot when you're anxious. They become easily irritable, snapping at the slightest provocation because they're already a big bundle of tense nerves, to begin with. If you find yourself easily irritable, angry, or emotional at the drop of a hat, the chances are you're overwhelmed by your emotions and probably feeling anxious thanks to all the excessive thoughts running wild in your head.

To Fight or Take Flight?

This response is the reason behind the out of body experience you sometimes go through when you're feeling extremely anxious. It is your body's way of coping by removing the excess stimuli that it thinks is too much for you to handle. Our fight-or-flight response is a reaction to stress, and this is a reaction that most likely evolved out of the survival needs from our early ancestors who lived in dangerous times. Our early cavemen ancestors were in constant danger of animals. One minute they might be lighting a fire, and the next minute, there's a stampede coming their way, and they need to evacuate as soon as possible. The human body's natural survival design then kicks in, and we have a full surge of energy and strength to quickly respond to the threat by removing ourselves from danger and increasing our chances of survival. Even though it is a survival mechanism, your body is not meant to remain in this state of alertness for long. All that cortisol pumping through your body will eventually take its toll on your mental, physical, and emotional health.

Am I An Introvert? Or Is It Anxiety?

An introvert is someone who prefers their own company. When you're an introvert, you consider yourself someone who is reserved and quiet. There is nothing wrong with being an introvert. Not in the least, since it takes all sorts of personalities to create this beautiful, diverse world we live in. Imagine if we lived in a world where everyone was an extrovert? There wouldn't be any balance, and it would be hard to find time for yourself if people always love to talk, talk, talk. But even introverts can be confident when they need to rise to the occasion. This is not the case when someone is dealing with social anxiety.

If it is anxiety or social anxiety (the more serious variant) that you're dealing with, you have an intense fear of social situations. The very idea of being around people, particularly people you don't know, *terrifies you*. It makes you so anxious that, depending on your fear level, you could induce a panic attack and start hyperventilating at the very thought of social situations. Social anxiety is a disorder, and the official acronym for it is *SAD (Social Anxiety Disorder)*. SAD can manifest in several ways, from shyness and nervousness to dreading everyday activities because it means you need to be around people. Whenever you know you have to go out in public, you start sweating and feeling nervous, like your heart is racing a mile a minute. These anxious heart palpitations can make it feel like it's hard to breathe sometimes.

The problem with SAD is that, like anxiety in general, it can be attributed to a number of factors. An even bigger problem is the way that it can affect your physical and mental health, and of course, your confidence along with it. It's hard to feel like a confident person when nervous beads of sweat keep dripping off your forehead, and you feel like you can't stop shaking and trembling. SAD could be caused by the way your brain is genetically structured, a traumatic event you went through in life, your environment and upbringing, the list could keep going. Let's take a closer look at the difference between someone who is an introvert and someone who struggles with SAD:

An introvert is:
- A person who is focused on themselves and their mental state of health.
- Usually perceived as someone who tends to focus inwards and look within themselves to find the answers they seek.
- A person who likes to spend time alone because they feel like it helps them recharge their batteries.
- A person who prefers their own company. They would prefer to be at home curled up with a good book rather than be out partying with a group of strangers.
- A person who actively seeks solitude to reconnect with themselves. In fact, they find these moments of solitude rewarding.
- Someone who is not against being social, but they are particular about who they would prefer to spend their time with.
- A person who enjoys doing things by themselves in the comfort of their own home.

- A person who is selective about the circle of friends and people they choose to keep close to them. They usually have a few good people in their life with whom they share a strong bond.

An anxious person is:
- A person who is frightened of social events to the point that they sometimes turn down invitations because they can't deal with the stress. It is not that they would rather be at home, but they're paralyzed by their fears.
- A person who feels uneasy at the thought of being around people. They might get nervous butterflies in their stomach or feel queasy and lightheaded from all that stress.
- A person who doesn't like being out in social situations because they are always worried about how others are perceiving them. They worry if people are talking about them behind their backs. They worry if people think poorly of them.
- A person who feels dread when things are not in their control. This explains why they hate social events. They can't control how the event is going to go, how their interactions with other people are going to go, and they can't control the outcome of what might happen at those events. This makes them extremely nervous, and they feel vulnerable and exposed.
- A person who struggles a lot internally since they can't make their fears known to anyone. They're too afraid of being perceived as weird, and the truth is, not everyone is going to understand what it is like to live with anxiety all the time.
- A person who might have become so reclusive that they don't go out and do things anymore unless they are left with no other option.
- A person who becomes distressed when they find themselves being in a situation where they are the center of attention. They become distressed when they feel they are being watched or observed while they are doing something.
- A person who becomes distressed when they feel insecure and out of place in social situations, very often uttering the phrase I don't really know what to say.
- A person who feels distressed and constantly wants to withdraw from the limelight to avoid any unwanted attention.
- A person who doesn't enjoy the activities that they used to anymore because every social event feels daunting.
- A person who struggles to maintain relationships.
- A person who becomes distressed, nervous, and visibly awkward and uncomfortable when being introduced to new people.

For those struggling with anxiety, confidence is almost nonexistent. They can leave messages unread for days, emails unanswered, phone calls not returned for no specific reason. Most of the time, they try to avoid any possibility of conflict, and if their anxiety is bad enough, they leave messages unanswered for days simply because they are worried the conversation could be a bad one. When you're dealing with anxiety or its more severe form, SAD, you find yourself experiencing feelings of fear, apprehension, and nervousness, often prominent when you think that you might be put in a social situation in which you could possibly do something humiliating and embarrassing. For example, if you had to enter a room in which everyone is already seated down, and they are the last one to arrive, you fear that you could possibly trip and fall over and even worse, everyone in the entire room will take notice and laugh at them, a thought which is completely mortifying.

Dealing with nervous anxiety is not fun. Dealing with SAD is not fun either. How do you become a confident person when you're struggling to remain calm in the presence of others? How do you become a confident person when you dread the thought of being around people? SAD can eventually lead to loneliness and isolation because of the constant avoidance of human interaction. Those who live with SAD don't necessarily experience these feelings only when they are thrust into a new environment or situation. Sometimes the symptoms can even manifest themselves in familiar situations too, even around family and friends whom you are familiar with. Certain types of anxiety, like SAD, can be a chronic disorder, to a point where even everyday interactions cause extreme amounts of anxiety, fear, self-consciousness, and embarrassment because you fear being judged and scrutinized by others, even though they aren't necessarily doing it. SAD, in its chronic form, can result in it disrupting your daily routine, work, school, and any other activities because you feel like you can't cope well enough to perform those activities.

It's hard to be a confident person when anxiety turns you into someone who is in constant need of reassurance all the time. Anxiety sufferers don't seek out praise and recognition. When you're dealing with anxiety, you'll seek out reassurance to the point you might become obsessed with it. Anxiety sufferers continually seek validation and approval, wondering if what they did was good enough. Did I do this okay? Was this good? Did I mess up? Did I say or do something that might have offended someone? Was it okay to do that? Was it okay to say that? That's not the mark of someone who is confident. Not even a little bit. Anxiety will make you the opposite of what a confident person should be. You find it hard to trust your own judgment, and you're always double-checking and wondering, seeking reassurance that you're okay. You'll get stuck in your, unable to move onto the next task until you get the recognition you need to feel better about yourself.

Calming the Mind, Body, and Soul

When anxiety strikes, it is best not to think about being confident just yet. Instead, focus on calming your mind, body, and soul first before you attempt to do anything else. Those who deal with anxiety tend to have increased or heightened levels of arousal where their body is tense and on edge because of the stress hormones pumping through their veins at the time. Your mind and body are already going through a lot when you have to deal with something like this, and confidence is going to be the last thing on your mind. You need to try and take some deep breaths and do your best to calm your mind and body down. Understandably, this seems impossible unless you've got the right coping strategies to help you do it. What you need to do is arm yourself with one or two of the strategies from the list below and use them as your go-to options whenever anxiety rises within you.

A muscle relaxation technique that works really well when you're feeling nervous or anxious is called the *Progressive Muscle Relaxation Technique.* Using this technique, you would focus on taking deep breaths in and out. Each time you exhale, focus on releasing one muscle area of your body. Start by breathing in deeply, and on the exhale, loosen the muscle in your shoulder area as the air flows out of your body. Take another deep breath in, and on the exhale, relax your arms right down to your fingers. Repeat the process and go through all the areas of your body where you feel tense, progressively relaxing your muscles along the way. Once you've slowed down your racing mind, the next step is to regulate your emotions. This can be accomplished through mindfulness. Pay attention to the thoughts that run through your mind and the way your body is responding to them. That's the first step in taking control. Instead of letting the emotions go wild and unruly, pause and mindfully reflect on how you feel the impact it has on you. If your stress is making your shoulders hurt, take a few deep breaths and mindfully allow your body to relax.

How to Be Confident Even If You're Dealing with Anxiety

Depending on the severity of the anxiety you experience, there are ways you can work around your nervousness to appear confident, even if you might not be feeling 100% confident as yet. The trick is to give your mind something else to focus on besides how nervous you feel. Contrary to what you might think, you don't need as much confidence as you think. You can still *appear* to be confident even if the butterflies in your stomach are flapping their wings rapidly. If you give your mind something else to focus on, you can change the way that you think about your fears. Let's look at this example to illustrate that point. Imagine you are faced with a new challenge. You need to meet someone new, and this usually generates a lot of worry, fear, and anxiety for you. You worry that you might run out of things to say. You're worried you might not have anything in common to talk about. You're worried there might be too many awkward pauses in the conversation that make both you and the other person nervous. The anxious mind has a lot of worries that it could latch on to, and it does this because there is nothing else to focus on. No anchor point that it can use to steady itself.

In your mind, you are not brave enough to meet that new person for the first time. You think there is too much pressure involved, and you're worried you can't do it. Your anxiety will get the best of you unless you start shifting the way that you think. For example, you don't need to worry about the *entire* conversation all at once. All you need to focus on is the very start of the conversation; the part where you introduce yourself with a firm handshake, and a smile on your face. For any challenge, getting started is always the hardest part. But once you have got over this initial hump, everything quickly moves along. If you can muster up enough courage to take the first step and overcome that first big obstacle, then you know that you can handle anything that follows after that.

If you don't feel confident enough yet to face your social anxieties, there is nothing to worry about. Like everything else in this process, building that confidence is going to take time and practice. Practice makes perfect, and the following strategies are going to help you work on your confidence while still giving the impression that you are, well, not nervous at all:

- **Don't Make It Obvious That You're Not Confident** - Here's a secret you might not have thought about. *Nobody knows that you're not confident UNLESS you make it obvious.* Do you find yourself apologizing for being shy or lacking confidence? Well, it is time to stop doing that. You don't need to apologize for being shy or lacking confidence when there is a lull in the conversation or when you feel like things are getting awkward. That is *announcing* the fact that you're not a confident person. *No one has to know* unless you tell them or make it apparent. To you, it might be obvious that you're one big ball of anxiety, but to everyone else, you're a regular Joe like the rest of them. If you shout it from the rooftops, everyone is going to know about it. But if you play to cool and present a calm exterior without letting on how nervous you are, no one is ever going to know that you're silently working on overcoming your anxiety *except you*. People are not going to notice unless you tell them. If you apologize for being "shy" or "awkward," you are giving other people a label. They can use this label to define or identify you with, and it's going to be difficult to overcome that perception if you want them to see you as a confident person later on. Apologizing for your shyness or lack of confidence is going to completely change the other person's perspective. If they didn't see you as shy before, they will now.

- **There's No Need to Set the Bar Too High** - Being confident does not mean you need to be the most outgoing person in the room. Being confident does not mean you have to dominate every single conversation you have. You can be confident and still be a good listener, letting the other person do all the talking if you wanted. Setting the bar too high will only make each social interaction seem more intense than it really is. You're psyching yourself up unnecessarily when you do that. There is no need to be a perfect conversationalist to be considered a confident person. No one is expecting you to jump from being shy to immediately extroverted when you're around people. You are the only person putting this unnecessary expectation on yourself. It's okay not to raise the bar high. When you're playing a game of tennis for the first time, you don't pick up a racket and immediately expect to play as well as the professionals do. Even more so if you have never held a ball before. There's no need to leap too far ahead of yourself. Before you can become good at tennis, you need to work on improving your swings and hits before you can start thinking about power and control. It works the same way with your conversations. If you want to learn to overcome your anxiety and become a more confident person, start by lowering the bar that you have set for yourself, and then work your way up from there. When you meet someone for the first time, keep your conversations simple and to the point. Short and sweet. It may not be the most exciting conversation in the world, but it is a start, and it is an opportunity for you to practice your conversational skills. If you know your anxiety is triggered when the bar is set too high, lower the bar and work your way up. You don't need to dazzle anyone with a stupendous story right away or charm them with irresistible charisma. Start with the basics, and you will be a confident conversationalist before you know it.
- **Watching Other People** - This strategy works best if you're in a room full of other people. Whenever you're feeling particularly anxious or nervous, pause and spend a few minutes watching the other people in the room. Focus on their body language, because it will tell you whether they're genuinely confident or not. Are they confidently making eye contact with the people they're talking to? Or are they staring into space or looking at the ground. Are they standing comfortably? Or does their body language give you the distinct impression that they would rather be anywhere else but here. It can be oddly comforting knowing that you're not the only person out there trying to be as confident as you can be.

Think you're alone when you're feeling anxious? Not at all; other people are probably in the same boat you are, except that no one is talking about it out loud. Everyone is trying to be the best version of themselves they can be. You're not alone, and whenever you feel anxious, stop and watch the other people in the room. It might surprise you to learn that nine times out of ten, they are feeling as awkward or nervous as you are. We tend to assume that we are the only ones who are feeling socially awkward and struggling with nervous anxiety. We assume that everyone around us is brimming with the confidence we wish we had. The people who genuinely love attention are only a small and select group. The rest of us tend to feel awkward, shy, and a little bit nervous when we're faced with the prospect of being in a room full of people we don't know well. By watching other people, you can take comfort in the knowledge that you are not alone. People don't seem as intimidating when you know that they share the same fears you do.

- **Own Your Nervousness** - Being nervous and anxious is nothing to be ashamed of. In fact, you should feel *proud of yourself*. Here you are, struggling with nervous anxiety, and yet you're still willing to try. You're willing to be brave and give it your best shot, and that is something not a lot of people can say that they have done. Most people might not notice how shy or nervous you are, but once in a while, someone might call you out on it. They might say something like, *"You're kind of nervous/shy."* For most socially anxious people, their first instinct is to immediately apologize for the way that they are. *You don't have to apologize.* This does not have to be something that you are ashamed of. Your shy and anxious nerves can only define you if you allow it to. What you should do instead the next time someone happens to point out you're shy or nervous is *yes, I guess I am at times*. Your nervousness does not have to define your entire personality. It is merely a small part of who you are as a person. Because that is what it is. Your nervous anxiety does not define who you are. It is only a *small part* of who you are.

CHAPTER 4
Stomping Out Your Inner Critic

No one cares about what you have to say. You're a fraud, and they will see right through you. Everyone is going to see how nervous you are in the presentation. Nobody likes you, and you know it. You're a loser; you can never get anything right. You look ugly in everything you wear. None of your clothes fit right. You've got a massive pimple on your face, and everyone is going to be staring at it. How would you feel if someone was constantly criticizing your every move? Telling you things like, "You're so stupid! You're weird! You're never going to be good enough! You're ugly!" What if there was someone standing in front of you right now criticizing you to your face? Would you stand for it? Probably not. If they push your buttons enough, you're going to fight back and stand up for yourself. From the outside, these seem like hurtful, sometimes almost cruel remarks that someone might say to you. But what if you were told that *you* were the one saying these things? Your first reaction might be to recoil in horror at the thought. You could never imagine yourself saying such things to anyone, let alone the people you cared about.

But it's true. *No one is saying these things to you. You're saying them to yourself.* You know you are a nice person, and you know you would never say these things to other people. *Yet, you would say them to yourself without a second thought.* You definitely wouldn't let anyone talk like that to any of your loved ones, family, or friends. So why would you tolerate this level of unkindness from the voice inside your head? We say such awful things to ourselves all the time, and if you're struggling with confidence, you know that you are definitely guilty of saying mean and nasty comments to yourself all the time. We've become so used to saying these nasty comments to ourselves that we don't notice them anymore. They've become almost like a bad habit. This is a habit at least 99% of the world's population are guilty of. The other 1% are the ones busy being successful.

Your Unhelpful Inner Friend

Imagine you had a friend who was by your side 24-hours a day, 7-days a week. Imagine if this friend went on and on all day long saying negative, unhelpful, hurtful things to you. Imagine this voice constantly whispering to you that you are never good enough, and you're not fooling anyone with that bravado. *You're not good enough. You're not smart enough. You're not talented enough. You're not skinny enough.* All-day long it goes on and on like this. With everything that you want to do, this voice is right there by your side, pointing out all the ways you could possibly fail and fall flat on your face. That, my friends, is your inner critic.

It also happens to be the difference between people who are confident and people who are still struggling to build confidence. The former has already learned how to control their inner critic and its self-destructive nature. If you let that little voice be stronger than your belief in yourself, you are going to have a very tough time crawling out of your insecurity hole. As for everyone else? Well, we're still struggling with our inner critic to a certain extent. Give your inner critic enough power, and it *will overpower you*. The inner critic is made up of negative thoughts, beliefs, and attitudes that oppose our best interest and diminish our self-esteem. It is our own worst enemy.

Everybody has an inner critic. That is no exception. Even the successful people have it, except that they have mastered several ways to tune this critic out, ignore it, or get rid of it entirely. Why is the inner critic your unhelpful inner friend? Because if you let that little voice be more potent than your belief in yourself, you are going to have a very tough time crawling out of your insecurity hole. We all have a nasty little inner critic that lives somewhere in our mind, and if we let it out, listen to it and start to believe everything that it tells us, we're in big trouble. If you listen to this voice, you might try to push harder and try *too hard* to prove that voice wrong that you end up burning yourself out. You end up sabotaging your relationships, perhaps even your mental and physical well being too. If you're not careful, listen to this inner voice long enough, and it is like a one way trip down the deep, dark tunnel of depression. Because you *will* end up pushing yourself too hard for one simple reason: *No matter what you do, your inner critic is going to convince you that it is never enough.* Even if you gave it 150% of your effort, your critic is going to convince you that you're still a loser. When you burn out from pushing your mind and body way too hard, your inner critic pops up and says, *"See? I told you that you're not good enough."* There's no winning with this voice. That's why they call it a critic.

Listen to this inner critical voice long enough, and you will eventually hit rock bottom. It is inevitable when all that negativity is swimming around in your head. That's not to say that your inner critic is *all bad*. Sometimes the little voice in your head can be helpful if your mindset is one that knows how to use this voice as motivation to make changes for the better. Like when your inner critic reminds you junk food is not good, or that you need to get up and start exercising if you want to look good at the family wedding next month. However, when it is not helpful, it can lead you down a dark and dangerous road. Sometimes, the little voice takes a nasty turn and does more harm than good, especially when it starts steering us towards the realm of excess negativity. When this happens, what we're engaging in is negative self-talk, and if you let it, it will bring you down so low you'll find yourself drowning in negativity with no help in sight. Depression, severe depression, chronic anxiety, a nervous system that is fried and in need of some serious care, those are all symptoms of what can happen when you listen to your inner critic for too long.

The Critic That Killed Your Confidence

If you let your inner critic run free, it will destroy your confidence even more, so if you're an emotional person. Being emotional can bring out your inner critic. We have a tendency to be hard on ourselves, and we feel like we have failed in some way. However, if you hope to master your emotions, you need to develop the confidence you need to become psychologically stronger. Being too hard on yourself will only make your emotions more difficult to regulate because you're constantly critical, and that makes your emotions fluctuate. What is even more dangerous is how being in this condition for too long will eventually lead to severe depression. The World Health Organization says that 300 million people right now are suffering from depression. Yes, this condition is a global health crisis.

The trouble is that we have become so accustomed to this inner critic's nasty whisperings that we don't even notice or pay attention to it anymore. We've become so used to hearing that voice that we don't think twice about it. Sometimes the monologue can even happen on autopilot, and the musings of your inner critic can sometimes sound like a critical friend or family member who admonishes you. Negative self-talk can come in several versions. In some versions, it sounds grounded. *"I'm not the best at this task, so perhaps I should let someone else take charge, so we don't compromise the outcome. I can never do anything right! I should just give up!."* It could even sound like you're realistically appraising the situation when you say, *"I didn't get an A on my science test again, I guess I'm not good at science after all,"* although this version could quickly morph into fantasies based on fear, such as *"I'll probably never get into college if I keep scoring low grades on my tests like this!"* Yes, your inner critic can be a contributing factor to your depression (if you are struggling with depression). Imagine the damage this can do to your confidence if you let it go on. There could be a lot of reasons that contribute to why our inner critic seems to want to tear down our confidence. The first point of assessment should be your upbringing. What kind of environment were you surrounded in? Did your parents support you? Listen to you? Engage with you? Or did they tell you to stop being silly or stop making mistakes whenever you messed up? Your upbringing and the kind of environment you were surrounded in and exposed to makes a difference. The biggest culprits that kill our confidence are sometimes our own family, but we don't see it, don't want to see it, or fail to realize it. Parents and family members do occasionally criticize, perhaps when the situation calls for it but being overly critical about almost everything the child does, even when you mean well, is not good. If you grew up in this kind of environment, nothing would ever be good enough. The parent may have the best intention at heart, believing that by doing this it will help to ensure that the child does not grow up making costly mistakes in the future, but being overly critical can backfire. It may cause the child to develop insecurities and an inner critic who is always harsh, never believing that they are good enough to do anything, which can cripple them in adulthood. This is why your inner critic is the critic that killed your confidence.

With your inner critic leading the charge, you're never going to feel confident enough to want to try anything new. This negative way that you speak to yourself is damaging you from the inside. You're never going to be confident enough to rise to the challenges you face. You're never going to be confident enough to meet new people. You're never going to be confident enough in a lot of things that you do. The inner critic is going to cripple your confidence, keeping you small, and stuck in fear. Your inner critic will always run the day until you stand up to it and say *ENOUGH*. The time to stand up and stomp on your inner critic is *now*. Do it before it has a chance to do any more damage.

Say *ENOUGH* Is Enough

Don't wait until your confidence levels drop so low that it is almost non-existent anymore before you try and do something about it. The only person who can cure you of your inner critic is *yourself*. Your inner critic's negative self-talk is the underlying problem, and to become more confident, that pernicious little voice in your mind must be silenced. Your inner critic does nothing but complain, put your down, and sow needs of negativity and doubt in your mind. You don't need all of that in your life, and it is not going to benefit you in any way. You don't need that nagging little voice reminding you of how it could all go wrong and listing the many reasons you might fail. Moving forward, that inner voice must be silenced. If you don't work on the underlying issue first, you're going to find yourself back in square one each time you try to move forward.

It is time that you cast your inner critic aside so your true, confident self can shine. It begins right here by identifying what your priorities are. Make it your priority right now to become a more confident person by silencing your inner critic. Use this priority as the anchor you hold onto when challenges start billowing past you, trying to turn your world upside down. When an obstacle hits and throws all your plans in chaos, it's easy to get swept up in a negative emotional storm if you have nothing to fall back on. Being unable to identify what your priorities are will only serve to make the situation worse than it actually may be. Yes, silencing your inner critic starts with a priority. That priority is the goal you want to accomplish. It serves as a reminder of why you are working hard to silence this very unhelpful friend in your head who has become a burden. A goal helps you stay on track when challenges are threatening to distract and misdirect you.

If you are wondering whether having a priority and a goal is necessary for this process to work, the answer is *YES*. You absolutely need this if this first step at addressing the underlying problem is going to work. Your inner critic may try to silence you and hold you back along the way, but your priorities and goals remind you of what you want to accomplish. This is the emotional support system you need to keep you staying in control. You can be surrounded by all the positivity in the world, but if you don't believe in yourself and your abilities, you're not going to go very far either. No matter what difficulties or challenges life may throw at you, remember you have the power within you to help you get through it. Part of becoming a more resilient person believes in yourself; after all, you've made it this far, haven't you? You wouldn't have if you weren't already a capable person.

The Power of Choice
Choice can be your most powerful weapon in your battle against your inner critic. In life, relationships, or work, challenges are a constant part of our life, and there will always be another challenge and another obstacle to face. But you always have a choice of how you want to react to it. It's not going to be easy, but it can be done, and that's what you need to keep reminding yourself each time you struggle to get past your inner critic. Imagine that you are now holding your hand out in front of you with your palm open and facing upward. Now, imagine that you are taking your inner critic, plucking it from your mind, and then placing it directly in the palm of your hand. Visualize this happening for a minute. Now, crush your inner critic by balling your hands tightly in a fist. Visualize yourself, *squashing it hard*. You're not ready to start crushing your inner critic.

How to Overcome Your Inner Critic for Good
Before you begin the strategies below to help you overcome your negative inner critic, there's something you need to be mindful of—your *thoughts*. Our thoughts are sometimes the things we pay attention to the least. Until they start getting out of control, that is. How easy it is for your negative thoughts to quickly start spiraling out of control before you know it. Negativity is like a disease. Once it gets a hold of you, it will do its best to keep hanging around, refusing to let go. The only way to start working on that challenge is to start practicing mindfulness and watch what you think. Recognize the kind of messages your brain is sending to itself. You might be taken aback to realize just how harmful a lot of the messages you send yourself are.

Don't let this internal enemy rob you of any more of your precious confidence and self-esteem. You are capable of great change, but the greatest change can only happen once a shift in the mindset takes place. The mind is a very powerful thing, and we can easily become a prisoner of our thoughts without even realizing that it is happening until it is too late. But that means that our minds are just as capable, just as strong enough to turn things around if we wanted it to. It's time to turn the tables on your inner critic, and this is what you need to do:

- **Turn Your Critic Into A Character** - Visualize your inner critic again as a separate entity. Imagine that they were not living inside your head. Imagine they were a real person. Who is your inner critic? What do they look like? Are they male or female? Tall? Short? Imagine your inner critic in such detail that they almost become like another person altogether. Turning your inner critic into a character is an important step in shutting it down for good because when you imagine your inner critic as someone else, you can slowly begin distancing yourself from them. In the same way, you would stay away from a toxic person. Your confident self and your inner critic cannot co-exist. They must become two separate entities if you want to become a more confident person.
- **Fight Back Against Your Inner Critic** - Don't let your inner critic walk all over you. Don't let it convince you that you're not good enough or worthy. Whenever your inner critic tries to say something that tears down your confidence, fight back against it with one very simple question: *Why?* Each time you have a bad thought, stop and ask your critic why? What evidence do you have that will lead you to believe what your critic is trying to convince you of. You'll need to put on your analytical thinking cap here and fight your inner critic with good old fashion logic. Criticizing yourself is something you've done long enough. This time, it's time to fight your critic in the form of questions. It might surprise you to find the more you try to justify your negative thoughts with evidence or facts, the more you'll struggle. Why? Because what your inner critic is trying to convince you of is *not* based on facts. It's not real. As your inner critic stumbles and fumbles, trying to find an answer to your rebuttals, it's time to move onto the next point.
- **Slamming the Door Shut** - Remember how you're supposed to picture your inner critic as a separate person? Well, this is where you get to have a little bit of fun. If you have always wondered what it feels like to slam the door shut on someone you disliked, now is your chance to do it. Well, not really, but close enough. Slamming the door shut on your inner critic is going to feel so good. It helps if you imagine your inner critic as an annoying salesperson who comes knocking on your door at the most inconvenient times. You would tell them, *"Nope, sorry, not interested,"* and close the door. Do the same thing to your inner critic. Slam the door shut on this annoying entity that is trying to steal your confidence. Your inner critic is knocking on your

mental door, coming to plant these seeds of doubt, hoping to steal your confidence away. What are you doing? Getting ready to slam the door shut. That is what you are doing.

- **Replace Your Negative Thoughts Like You Replace Old Clothes** - Toss them out. Toss them out by replacing your negative thoughts with a positive one instead. For every negative thought you have, think *two* happy thoughts to counteract it. This is the only effective technique needed to squash that inner critic inside you. If you don't do anything about it, the negative thoughts in your head are only going to steadily ruin your success a little bit at a time if you don't do something to stop it. It's important to start acknowledging what you say to yourself. You're doing it all the time anyway, except we're not mindful of these thoughts. Listen to the way you talk to yourself. Identify what your unhelpful thoughts are and separate them from the negative ones. Yes, there is a difference between the two. Not all negative thoughts are necessarily bad. An example of a negative thought is, *"I'm stressed and frustrated, but I know it will get easier,"* while an unhelp thought would be, *"I hate my current job, and I never want to go back to that office again!"* Once you begin noticing the messages you send, it's time to replace the less than desirable ones. What you could do, for example, is choose to either see a setback as a failure or acknowledge that they can sometimes be opportunities in disguise. Instead of seeing failure as an indication that you're not good enough, see failure as a teacher you learn from. It all depends on how you look at it. Train your mind to look at this from a positive point of view. See the bright side and the good of every situation, and you will find that often things may not be as bleak as it initially seems. You need to start paying attention to your thoughts because this is where you start making the necessary changes needed to change the way you think. When we're not mindful of the changes in our thoughts, the negativity makes us feel worse, and it becomes even more difficult to focus. By paying attention to the thoughts that creep into your head, you're instantly more attuned to what those thoughts are and how they make you feel. If it is bad for you or going to affect your confidence levels, you need to remove these thoughts from your life for good.

- **Focusing on Nothing But the Facts** - Once again, facts are going to be your greatest weapon in this step. If a thought is not valid and based on facts, push back against these thoughts by focusing on the information that you know. Always go back to the facts that you know and cross-reference that with your thoughts. Ask yourself, "Am I basing this on fact? Or speculation?". Replace these unhelpful thoughts with concrete facts to support your argument and make it believable. The facts never lie, and focusing on this is one way of reigning in your thoughts to keep them from spiraling out of control. Reframe your mindset to look at the areas of your life or your personality that you are not satisfied with just yet and think about what you can do to change that. Instead of beating yourself up and letting your inner critic put you down, challenge yourself to think about how you can change those areas, and start believing in yourself. Believe in your abilities. Believe that this stressful period is not going to last forever. The storm will pass, and you need to believe you are strong enough to stick it out.

- **Love Yourself -** Love yourself enough to the point that you feel guilty for even thinking about these bad thoughts about yourself. Be happy and satisfied with who you are—choosing to be happy means being okay with where you are in life, even if it is not necessarily where you want to be just yet. The answer to that is much easier when you've identified a sense of purpose, something you can use as an anchor that keeps you rooted and wavering so your stress will never get the best of you. You can certainly get through anything with the right attitude and positive beliefs backing you up. If you could do it then, there is nothing stopping you from doing the same thing again except a whole bunch of excuses your inner critic has just fed you with. You need to love yourself, or rather, learn to love yourself again because you are worth it, and your inner critic has made you forget who you are and how much you are worth. Are you going to let your negative emotions and thoughts define who you are and dictate what your life should be? Or do you want more out of this one life that you have to live? Loving yourself is the only way you're ever going to have the courage to be brave enough to stand up for yourself. If you don't love yourself, you're sending a clear message to your inner critic that you're easily dominated. You need to love yourself first and foremost and use the strength of that love to help you develop your confidence. A person who loves themselves will never allow themselves to be treated with anything less than respect. The decision is yours to be as positive or as negative as you want to be in the face of stress.
- **Be Comfortable Talking About Your Feelings -** Don't forget that the brain has a limited storage space capacity. All those thoughts need to go somewhere, or they're going to get bigger and bigger, making it feel like your head is about to explode at the next trigger. Even if those emotions are uncomfortable or something you would prefer not to deal with, do it anyway because it is still a part of who you are. It can be hard to remain positive all the time, especially when you've experienced a setback or things are

not going according to plan. When you let your emotions out, you're going to feel so much better. Like a huge weight has been lifted off your chest. Talking about things can be a very liberating feeling. It is time you started living the life that you were meant to live. Don't be afraid to talk about your emotions when you need to. Don't be afraid to talk about your emotions. Don't keep your emotions bottled up inside. Learn to be okay with expressing yourself and letting it all out. Your emotions are not your enemy, so start embracing them instead of resisting them. One of the unspoken things we yearn for is a deep connection to others. But in order to develop that deep connection, we must be able to openly share ourselves with others. We need to build enough trust to let others in, or we will always feel alone.

- **I Don't Have to Be Perfect** - Let this be the answer you always give your inner critic from now on when it tries to convince you that you're not worth it. Push back against your inner critic with this sentence whenever it tries to tell you that you're going to fail if you try. *You don't have to be perfect.* No one in this world is perfect, not even the successful people out there today. They've all failed and fallen several times along the way, made mistakes they wished they hadn't, but they still didn't let their inner critic stop them or rob them of their confidence. Why? Because they knew that they did not have to be perfect. You don't have to be perfect before you're worthy of love. You don't have to be perfect before you can strike up a conversation with someone. You don't have to be perfect before you start going after that promotion at work that you want. *You don't have to be perfect because no one is.* Let that sink in and let that be one of the anchors you hold onto whenever your inner critic tries to lead you astray. You are doing your best, and that is all anyone can do.

Preaching Positivity

In fact, why not take a leaf out of the motivational speaker's book and do what they do? At every opportunity, jump at the chance to talk about positivity. Imagine you're like a motivational speaker, and it's now your mission to spread positivity at every chance you get. Especially when you're interacting with someone who needs it and who may be struggling to overcome negativity too, you may not be a motivational speaker in a professional capacity, but that doesn't mean you can't take a leaf out of their book and preach and teach too. If your mind is capable of complaining and being negative without even thinking about it, you can certainly change your brain and your thoughts, so it goes in the opposite direction too.

If you think you can't be a positive person because of the mistakes you have made, *think again*. The control is always in your hands, and the way you feel says a lot about what you choose to focus on. Focus on your strengths and all the other trials you've managed to overcome before. You got through those, and you are much stronger because of it. Remember, all you can do is your best, and you need to let that be enough. Look at it this way, if you tried and you failed, that means you were *brave enough* to try and do something. That is something you should absolutely be proud of. You may not have succeeded today, but the point is that you tried, and that is something your inner critic can never take away from you.

CHAPTER 5
Building A Tougher Character

Are you resilient? After you get knocked down, do you pick yourself back up? Getting back up on your feet again after a particularly tough challenge is not always the easiest thing in the world. In fact, it is going to feel like a nearly impossible task if you don't have a tough character alongside confidence. Mentally tough and resilient people don't happen overnight, and they don't magically appear one day. Nor were they born with it. It is a quality which they worked hard at building every day to get to where they are right now. It took hard work, self-discipline, willpower, and the determination to never back down and never say die. When things got tough, they took that as an opportunity to prove to themselves just what they were made of, and over time, the resilience and toughness became a part of who they were. But if you ask them whether it was all worth it, their answer will always be a resounding *yes*.

When you've got a tough character and confidence on your side, you're much happier. You're happier because you are not afraid to go after what your heart desires. You're happier because you're willing to take risks, and you know that nothing feels better than seeing those risks pay off in a big way. You're happier because you're not afraid to go out there and live the life that you want on your own terms. You're happier because you are not afraid of failure anymore when you know how to stand up again every time you've been knocked down. You're happier because you have the confidence and the resilience to do all of the above and so much more. Resilience and confidence are life-changing traits you can and should be focused on developing.

Resilience and Why We Need It

If you dare to dream big and you want to go after your goals, you are going to fall down. Not once, not twice, but several times along the way before you can cross that finish line. You're going to cry, you're going to feel stressed and frustrated, and you're going to be pushed to your limits. That is because nothing that is worth having is ever going to come easily. You have to *earn* the life that you want, and it is going to push you to your breaking point. But if you can see it through and survive, everything is going to be worth the effort and the struggle. The problem is, it is hard to survive the emotional, mental, and sometimes physical turmoil that these challenges will present you with if you are not mentally tough, resilient, and confident.

The struggles are how you know that you are on the right track, that you are living your life to the fullest and going for the big goals. It is completely okay to fail. It is *good* if you fail once or twice along the way. The challenges are how you know that you are giving meaning to your life, that your life has a purpose and a goal. Where most of us struggle is how to pick ourselves back up again faster and with double the persistence. Staying stuck in the self-criticism and the self-doubt that these trials and tribulations will sometimes present you with are the reasons why you need a tougher character and confidence on your side. You do need failure, and you do need hardships because that is how we learn and grow. What you are trying to do now is figure out a way to bounce back quickly so you can keep the momentum going.

The easiest way to define resilience is the ability to bounce back to your original state after being put through the wringer. When challenges push you, pull you, stretch you, and turn your emotions upside down, that ability to quickly recover your focus and determination, that ability to keep going is how you define resilience. That is how you know you have a tougher character that won't quit at the first sign of hardship. A tough character gives you the ability to keep growing and keep putting one foot in front of the other when you feel like quitting the most. It is the discipline to stay focused despite what you may be going through and the determination to never give up.

What Resilient People Do

When they get their butts kicked, resilient and tough people, they embrace their emotions. When they get rejected and face disappointments, they embrace their feelings. They acknowledge all the emotions that may be running through them, and they embrace those emotions rather than deny them. It's natural to want to resist negative emotions. They're unpleasant, but you now need to embrace them just as you would with the emotions that make you feel good. Acknowledge that they're there, and don't fight it off. Resisting them will only diminish your confidence in your ability to remain in control, and a lack of confidence is going to work against you as an attempt to make progress. Resilient people don't jump immediately into thinking positively or using affirmations to help them let go of the hurt and pain they're experiencing. They take the time they need to embrace those emotions and process them properly.

When you try to move on too quickly, you're not addressing your emotions properly. You're numbing, repressing, or bottling up your emotions, and that is never a healthy thing to do. You need to create a safe space for yourself to feel these emotions, even if they are hard, and even if you don't want to think about them. Openly acknowledge that you feel the way you do; there's nothing to be ashamed of. Analyze and think about the significance of that emotion in relation to the situation that you find yourself in. Why do you feel this way? What has triggered such a response? When someone has made you angry, for example, instead of resisting the emotion, acknowledge your anger at the circumstances that triggered it. You are allowed to feel disappointed, hurt, and frustrated.

You are allowed to feel pain. Your emotions are not something to be ashamed of, even though some emotions are unpleasant to deal with.

Tough personalities embrace all of these emotions, good and bad, and they let them all in. The difference between them and other, less confident people, are that these tougher personalities don't wallow in their misery. They embrace it when the situation sucks. They embrace it when they feel hurt and disappointed. They embrace and then move on. How do they seem to move on without being stuck for too long? They know those feelings they have are temporary. They know the disappointment is temporary. They know that feeling hurt and pain is temporary. The only way those feelings are going to become permanent is if you allow them to stay. There is a quote that goes like this: *"Your emotions are like the waves of the ocean. You can't stop them from coming, but you can choose which wave you want to surf"*. This quote is a profound reminder that you will never be able to prevent your emotions, but you can choose how you're going to let it affect you. There is another old saying that goes: *"It's not what happens to you, but rather how you choose to respond to it that matters."* This is very true indeed. It is the way you have chosen to respond that has led you to this point in your life, where you are right now.

This is how confident people manage to stay resilient and tough, no matter what happens to them. They know that it comes down to learning how to regulate and master your emotions. It is what they do every single day and how they keep themselves ahead of everyone else. This is how they ensure that no matter what happens, they never let challenges rob them of their confidence. They observe their feelings and reflect on them. It is easy to fall out of touch with ourselves in this hectic world that we live in. With the hectic lives we juggle, trying to manage one thing after another, taking care of ourselves often falls by the wayside, and we lose that connection to our innermost feelings. The way you chose to respond was influenced by your perception and interpretation of the circumstances that happened in your life. When you're unable to manage your emotions properly, that's when you make impulsive decisions that often result in regret later on.

Mentally tough and resilient individuals never get stuck in their emotions for too long because they know the discomfort is not going to last. They know that they will move through whatever it is they are feeling, and they will be stronger because of it. This knowledge helps them stay calm enough to keep themselves focused on the bigger picture and keeps their confidence intact. What most people choose to do is the easier, more convenient thing. Instead of learning how to focus on their emotions, they choose to brush it aside, ignore, or deny their emotions completely. They may even distract themselves from those feelings by doing something else. The more you deny your feelings, though, the harder it becomes to manage them later on. Bottling up your emotions and hoping they will just go away on its own has never proven to be an effective strategy. If it were, there would be no such thing as emotional outbursts. Another thing that resilient people do is show understanding, compassion, and kindness to themselves. They don't have themselves for having these emotions. They're *kind* to themselves *because* they have these emotions. They don't take pity on themselves or think of themselves as the victim, which is what most other people tend to do. Feeling sorry for yourself when your emotions have gotten out of hand is not beneficial. Yes, you feel sorry and regret what's been done. You wish you would have handled the situation better, but feeling sorry for yourself is not going to change what has happened. Negativity will one serve to make your emotions spiral even more out of control than they already are. Things always seem ten times when you're down in the dumps, so it's time to get rid of this habit and start taking accountability for your emotions.

Resilient and confident people are never looking to shift the blame. They never try to point the finger or blame someone else for the way they feel. If you're always looking for an opportunity to blame someone else, to eagerly shift the blame, so you don't have to feel as bad about losing control, you need to keep working on your emotional intelligence as well as your confidence. The way you choose to react is always a decision that lies with you. No one forced you into it; that was completely your decision and yours alone. Resilient and confident people show understanding toward themselves. They understand that they are allowed to feel disappointed and frustrated sometimes, and it is okay to feel everything that they feel. They love themselves enough to treat themselves with kindness and to treat themselves with kindness, even in the face of disappointments. It is not a bad thing to love yourself, and no one should make you feel guilty about it. If you are going to constantly rely on others to feel worthy, you will never become the improved version of yourself that you long to be. Self- love is not to be confused with narcissism. Narcissism is being in love with yourself, which is a different matter altogether. Self-love is a reminder to yourself that you're good enough the way you are, and you deserve to have good things happen to you too. If you have no problem telling people you love how amazing and incredible they are, and how deserving they are of love, why not do the same for yourself? For happiness to exist long-term, self-love needs to be present.

Confidence Requires Mental Toughness

When the going gets tough, it can be tempting to give in to the desire to quit, admit defeat, and run away. But those are the instincts you need to battle against, and it is a battle you must not lose. The minute you do, your hope of being tougher mentally diminishes just a little bit more with each defeat. Do not give in to fear, because you are capable of so much more than you give yourself credit for; you have overcome difficult situations in the past, you need to now make it a habit of doing it all the time.

Resilience Is A Character Trait

There are several phrases that could be used to describe someone. Hard-working, generous, compassionate, friendly, honest, wise, confident, and the list goes on. If you were to describe yourself in one word, what would it be? Is it a description that you would be happy to be associated with? Picture your ideal self. Visualize it as though it has already happened, and you are the person that you want to be. What values do you see yourself having? If you were looking at yourself from a third-person point of view, would you be happy with the character traits that you see? Be crystal clear about the vision, and it will help you believe that you are everything that you want to be. Building a tougher character means never giving in to the urge to run away when things get hard.

Resilience Is Built Through A Willingness to Change

Bruce Lee, one of the most famous martial artists in history, was known for encouraging his students and followers to emulate water. While most people saw water as a sign of weakness, Lee, on the other hand, saw water as the ultimate sign of strength. He was always encouraging everyone to be just like water because water can never be snapped. In his own words, Lee said that everyone should be like water because it is soft, resilient, and formless. Water was one of the strongest existing elements here on Earth because of its very nature and ability to move, adapt, and elude when needed. Instead of fighting and resisting, water adapts.

Lee was always someone who was determined to look forward and keep moving, just like water did. Lee was someone who lived fiercely and intensely in his present moment. He was always working on improving himself by gathering experiences and knowledge that would help him grow into a better and wiser person. One of his philosophies was that a person needs to keep on flowing just like the water did because water that runs can never grow stale. Bruce Lee was a firm believer that everyone could learn to overcome the obstacles in the way that water did. Instead of fighting and resisting the challenges that come our way, Bruce Lee believed that we should embrace those challenges and learn to move alongside the obstacles that come into our path. It is only in this way that everyone could silently conquer their obstacles. Throughout his life, Lee based a lot of his philosophy on emulating the movement and the flow of the river. He never clung to the circumstances of his past; instead, he chose to let his current existence take him to unknown places because he was willing to adapt when he needed to. He never clung onto the past, or let it hold him back,

Resilience Is Built Through Gratitude
Being grateful helps remind you that you should stop and remember to live in the present. Not just live in the moment, but be grateful for it and everything good that has happened to you as of that moment. This is a complete opposite of what a lack of confidence will encourage. Poor confidence does nothing but plague you with stress and worries, whereas gratitude teaches and reminds you that you have a lot to be grateful for if you really think about it. When you have so much to be thankful and grateful for, worries and challenges seem to bother you a lot less. Not only does gratitude actively remind you of the things you have to be grateful for, but when you actively remind yourself of all the good experiences you have in your life, it eventually helps to magnify positive thoughts, and soon, the positive thoughts will eventually be strong enough to overpower any negative and toxic emotions that might be holding you back from becoming the confident person you should be. Be grateful every single day. It makes you tougher and less prone to stress.

Steps to A More Resilient and Confident You
Life is going to toss you all sorts of curveballs, and the only way you're going to make it through that with your confidence intact is if you work on becoming resilient and tough. Build that strong character that is going to make you as tough as nails. Tough enough to handle even the most difficult challenges you have ever faced up to this point. These steps are going to make a difference in your life, and this is what you need to do:

- **Develop A Positive Way of Talking to Yourself** - When things aren't going your way, and you are being pushed to your limits to the point of wanting to give up, *how do you talk to yourself through this tough time?* Do you motivate and encourage yourself? Treat yourself with kindness? Or do you kick yourself and tell yourself what a massive disappointment you are? What sort of language do you use when you're talking yourself through these tough times? The way you talk to yourself should be encouraging, motivating, and kind. It should use language that makes sense, a language that is compassionate. You're already feeling pretty terrible that something didn't work out the way that you hoped; you don't have to kick yourself when you're already down. You wouldn't kick someone else when they were already feeling at their lowest point, so why do it to yourself? Be *kind* because it goes a long way toward your self-esteem and confidence. Be kind because you don't deserve to be treated unkindly when you know you have already tried your best. When you've fallen, think about what you would love to hear from a friend or loved one. What could they say to you that would make you feel loved and supported during this tough time? *That* is the kind of language you should be using on yourself. You need to know how to pick yourself up again in the *right manner* whenever you have fallen because you are going to fall many times. It is going to get to you if you don't have a healthy coping mechanism. It's time to put the inner critic on mute and let your self-talk become emotionally empowering and inspiring instead. If you don't learn how to tune out the negative voice you might have become so accustomed to, your problems and challenges are always going to seem magnified and worse than they are. Everything is going to feel like a big deal when you don't have a healthy coping mechanism. Let the way you talk to yourself be filled with love and support.

- **Detach from Your Thoughts** - Your thoughts will take you on an emotional roller coaster if you leave them in charge. Your thoughts will try to convince you of things that aren't true. When your thoughts begin to feel like they're overpowering you, your sense of control begins to slip away, and that only causes you to feel even more frustrated and miserable at the way things are going. Your thoughts are always going to try and play tricks on you because that is what your inner critic loves to do. Play games with your mind and convince you that all your worst fears are true, and there is nothing you can do to change that. Your mind is your most powerful weapon of change to achieve success in everything that you do in life. If you want your life to change, to think better, do better, and achieve more, then you need to begin taking ownership of your thoughts and change the way you think. Nothing is going to change unless you make the choice to do it. To be accountable and take ownership of your mind and your thoughts. To be a problem solver instead of a downer and changing your mindset is what you need for change is going to get you there. Reframing your point of view is essentially changing your mindset. A mind over matter exercise. If you put your mind to it, you can do it. *Your feelings are not facts. They are your emotions.* Emotions are volatile, and they will shift and change at the drop of a hat. Why allow yourself to believe these thoughts are true? It is only going to distress you if you do. You need to learn to detach from your thoughts. Your negative thoughts do not define who you are and what you can do. Don't give them this kind of power over you and your confidence. You don't need to take your thoughts seriously. You don't need to pay attention or engage with every thought that pops into your head, especially if the negative ones. You don't need to perceive every thought you have is the truth. You are not your thoughts. You don't have to ignore or deny your thoughts, but don't let yourself get swept up by them until you start losing confidence.

- **Minding Your Language** - Let's dig a little deeper about the language we use when we're going through particularly tough times. The language that we use most often determines our brain's fundamental capacities and the automatic physiological we are subjected to because of that language. Words can be a powerful force of good when used for the right reasons, but on the other end of the spectrum, it can be used to inflict great harm and pain. The old adage about how the pen is mightier than the sword stems from the very real fact that words can cause a great deal of pain and leave scars so deep they might never fully recover. English philosopher and writer Aldous Huxley once said words are like an X-ray. When words are used in negative ways, these words can pierce through almost everything. Dignity, self-esteem, even the identity of another can be threatened with the right kind of words. Being aware of the way we use our words is one of the most crucial factors that will determine the state of our emotional wellness. In other words, if you want to be happy, you need to be using the right words and language. We rely on language to interpret the different sensations, events, and experiences we undergo. We use language to put a name to the emotion that we're feeling at the time. The different words that we use create different physiological responses. For example, two people could be going through the same situation. When one person says, *"It could have been worse,"* while the other person says, *"This is the worst thing that could have ever happened to me."* The first individual is going to be the one with a better, slightly happier emotional well being by simply phrasing the same situation using different words. Rephrase the language you use so that you are embracing your emotions for what they are instead of trying to deny their presence. Use your words to understand your negative emotions instead of treating them like an enemy. Everything is temporary and impermanent, even your emotions, so mind your language to keep your confidence intact.
- **Accepting the Fact That Life *Is Hard*** - It may not be what you want to hear, but it is a fact you can't deny. Life is hard. Denying it is not going to make it any easier. Getting worked up over the hardship is not going to change anything. Life is hard, and it has its moments. Some people are going through harder times than others. Life is not perfect. Nobody is perfect, no matter how hard they try to make it seem like they are. Life is hard, and no one has an easy time of it. Everyone goes through hard times, and you're not alone in this. That's why self-love and self-acceptance can be a challenge. Hard times will definitely try to beat you down, and it takes a lot of courage and inner strength to push back against it. But if you believe in yourself, you're already

winning. Life will have its ups and downs. It is not always going to be hard, and it is not always going to be easy. That is the way it is, and the sooner we embrace it, the easier it will be when you're not pushing back, fighting, and resisting against life. Instead of being angry about it or hating it, embracing it will make you more willing to go through life. This willingness and open-mindedness is the key to staying focused and confident throughout the hard parts.

- **Be Responsible for Your Choices** - To overcome the victim mentality, you need to take a step back. One of the biggest challenges we all face is taking responsibility and being accountable for our own emotions and our choices. It is always easier to point the finger at someone else, to blame others, and claim they are responsible for what has happened. These options are easier than having to look inside ourselves and face the unpleasant fact that we may have a bigger role to play in our misery. Believing and blaming others for your misery is the easier pill to swallow rather than having to admit that you are the cause of your unhappiness. Bad things happen; that's a part of life and the way it works. Sometimes we see it coming, other times we don't. Bad things can happen to anyone, anytime, anywhere. However, believing that these thoughts are done to you will trap you in a victim mentality. It distracts you from the truth, which is that these patterns of thought are simply a matter of habit. The trouble is most people tend to be too harsh on themselves. You're not trapped in a prison; you're merely trapped in a bad habit. You see, the mind is like the needle of a compass. It can only point in a single direction at a time. This means that we're only meant to think and focus on one thought at a time. This fact is going to be the secret to successfully shifting your thoughts away from negativity because you cannot think of a negative and positive thought at the same time. The victim mentality will lead you to believe that the world is out to get you; everything always happens to you. The problem always lies outward, and you don't think about looking inward for a source and solution. A "victim" will go through their entire lives blaming someone else or something else for where they are in life. No surprise why this paradigm sits on the negative end. As long as you keep blaming something or someone else for what's going on in your life, you will never have the power to change it. As long as you keep blaming, your mind will never have enough power or resources to overcome negativity. *You always have a choice. Always.*
- **Be Willing to Be Uncomfortable** - It is the only way you are going to grow and learn. You cannot become a better version of yourself if you are not willing to go through a little bit of

discomfort. Life can't be smooth sailing all the way, although we certainly wished that it could. If you're not willing to put yourself through the discomfort in order to get better, then you're never going to get better. That is the simple truth. You can't let fear make your decisions for you. You're not living to your full potential when you allow fear to cripple your motivation. You're not living when fear stops you from learning and developing the new skills you need to grow as a person. You're not living when you make poor decisions based on your fearful emotions. *You need to make the best decisions for yourself.* Nobody likes going through hard times and challenges, but it is these challenges that make us who we are. Just remember that the difficulties you encounter in your life are not a threat. They may be uncomfortable, but they are not a threat. They may not be pleasant, but they are not a threat. If they are not a threat, they don't have the power to affect your confidence *unless* you allow them to.

CHAPTER 6
It's Okay To Look After Yourself

If you have ever compared yourself to someone else and felt bad about yourself, nod your head in agreement. If you decided that they were better than you and your confidence took a nosedive because of that comparison, nod your head in agreement. If you ever felt like you were never good enough when you look around at everyone else around you, nod your head. If you're not taking care of yourself and your happiness the way that you should be, nod your head.

When you're young, other people are in charge of looking after you. Parents, guardians, other family members, babysitters, teachers, aunts, uncles, and grandparents who would remind you to look after yourself. Get enough rest, make sure you're eating all your fruits and vegetables, staying safe; they would be there to remind you of these things because they were responsible for your wellbeing. They affirm us, so we believe we're good enough, and we have what it takes to succeed. They support us so that we have the happiest childhood growing up by making sure we are safe and healthy. They set boundaries for us to make sure we are protected. But who looks after our wellbeing once we hit adulthood? *You are*. You are now responsible for your own affirming words and thoughts. You are not responsible for making sure you are well looked after, that your boundaries are in place, so you're safe, protected, and happy. You are now responsible for your own needs. You are now responsible for being your own cheerleader, and if you neglect all of the above, your confidence is going to be one of the elements that suffer the consequences.

The constant comparison to others, trying to figure out where you fit in within your social circle, thinking about where your life is going and whether you're living your life to the fullest, all of those things can have a big impact on the way that we feel. The outside world is filled with a lot of stress, and if you don't do anything to look after yourself, that stress is going to take its toll on you.

What Does Self-Care Mean

This is not a new concept. In fact, it has been the buzzword for a while now, and you've probably heard this term several times. People talk about it all the time on social media, blogs, podcasts, motivational speeches, inspirational books, even among people you might know in general. The best way to define self-care would be a *"happy, healthy, functional, and productive relationship with yourself."* When you're in a relationship with a partner, you're always so eager and willing to do things for the relationship to keep it healthy and happy. Well, self-care is pretty much the same thing except this time, you're going to be doing all those things for *yourself*. This is a term we have been hearing a lot in recent years. Mostly because people are finally beginning to realize how important it is to do things for yourself.

Now, it is important to highlight here that self-care and *self-love* are not the same things. Self-care is about taking action to improve or preserve your health. It is about the things you do to make yourself feel better. Some examples of this could include self-pampering, taking a nap when you're tired, taking a bath, going for a massage. Self-love, on the other hand, is focused on your regard for your own happiness and wellbeing. It is the way you see yourself. Both of these are essential to your happiness, and you need both of them to become a more confident person. You need to do things to look after yourself, and at the same time, you also need to pay attention to how you see yourself, not how others perceive you. Your opinion of yourself needs to be entirely yours, not what other people say about you. Self-love and self-care are different for everyone, and it's easy to see why these two concepts could be mistaken for the same thing. *"I must love myself if I'm going to treat myself to a nice weekend relaxing at the spa."* Right? Not necessarily, though. You could be doing all those things to look after yourself but still be saddled with low self-esteem because you don't think you're worthy. Taking care of yourself does not mean you accept your flaws or where you are in life and how happy you are with your accomplishments. You could be treating yourself to all the self-care techniques in the world but still be filled with an emptiness inside. If you're struggling to think about at least 5 things that you love about yourself, you need to work on strengthening that self-love aspect too. You can't be confident if you don't genuinely love who you are.

Are You Looking After Yourself?

What do you do right now to take care of yourself? Do you practice self-care? Ask most people this question, and you might be met with vague answers like, *"I like to read if I have the time. I get a pedicure once in a while. I go to the gym and try to eat healthily. I like to binge-watch something on Netflix during the weekends and stay in my pajamas."* Some people might even give you a blank stare in response to that question about what you do to take care of yourself. Beyond the little things here and there that we do for ourselves occasionally, most of us are not that great at taking care of ourselves. We certainly don't do it enough on a daily basis, and when we do, *we feel guilty about it*. We feel bad for taking time off to look after ourselves, and this is a sign of poor confidence. When you believe that you are *not worth* spending the time and energy on, you're not a confident person. You're not someone who practices self-love because you feel bad about looking after yourself.

A sure sign that you're not practicing self-care the way that you should is when you're willing to do this for other people, even if it means neglecting your own needs. You'll do it for them, but if you had to do the same for yourself, you would feel bad about it. You would be reluctant to do it because it feels selfish. If someone you cared about asked you to do something for them, you would do it anyway, even if you didn't feel like it. When you're in a relationship with someone you love, you encourage them to be the best version of themselves every day. We do an excellent job of making sure that the people in our lives know without a doubt that they matter to us. But when it comes to ourselves, why does the love stop? Why do we choose to neglect the most important relationship of all? The relationship that we have with *ourselves*. Why are we so willing to affirm, nurture, and protect the people we love, but we don't do it for ourselves? When we were young kids, it never crossed our minds that we weren't worthy enough. We never thought that we were not worth it. We never questioned our own value and worth. But we do it as adults. Why? Because for some strange reason or another, we've been led to believe that self-care is *selfish*.

Is It Selfish?

Self-care is *not selfish*. You can't pour from an empty cup. Self-care is never a selfish thing, and it's time to drop this frame of mind. It is never going to do you any good to constantly compare yourself to others. Their story is not the same as yours. You have your unique offerings based on your strengths, and that's where you draw on your confidence to see it through. When you need a break or a time-out, take it. Don't hesitate, don't feel bad, don't dwell on the guilt you feel. There's no reason to feel guilty about taking the time you need to look after your mental, physical, and emotional wellbeing. When you need a time-out or some self-care, take it. Don't let anyone make you feel bad for taking the time to care for the most important person you know. *Yourself.*

Right now, *you* are the most neglected person that you know. When was the last time you did something for yourself without feeling guilty about it? Self-care is part of learning who you are and knowing when you need to step back and take a breath. What do you need to feel recharged and connected with yourself again? Spending a few hours in your favorite spot curled up with a book? A nice, warm bath at the end of a long day? Learning about yourself is going to be a tough journey, and it is important to practice self-care along the way. It keeps your thoughts from becoming scattered and erratic whenever you're feeling the stress. No one should have to be made to feel guilty about practicing self-care. Self-care is self-help. On every flight, as the plane is getting ready for take-off, the air stewards and stewardesses go through the steps of their safety demonstration. In it, they advise in the event of an emergency that you put your oxygen mask on first before assisting others under your care. The same thing works with self- help. Before you can help others, you need to help yourself first.

Self-care is often confused for selfishness or self-indulgence. This explains why we feel bad about doing something for ourselves. We think we're being selfish by putting our needs first, but nothing could be further from the truth. Self-care is neither of those things; it is a process of intentionally giving yourself the help that your mind, body, and soul needs. *It's okay* to give yourself the weekend to rest and recover from a busy and hectic week. This shouldn't be a process you only do once in a blue moon. Rest and relaxation is something that needs to be regularly. Every week, in fact. You spend a lot of the week working hard, sometimes pushing yourself beyond your limits. Your body and mind need time to recharge and recover after that, and this needs to become a self-help habit you make part of your regular ritual. *It's okay* to do what makes you feel good, because why not? Thinking we "don't deserve it" is the wrong mentality to adopt. It is not going to do you any favors if you keep feeling guilty each time you do something for yourself. It's time to start believing that you are worthy. Feeling good about yourself yields important mental and physical health benefits. When we feel great, we're less stressed, and our mental and physical health doesn't suffer the consequences as much. Kindness and self-compassion are two important self-care qualities that you need to adopt. No one else can do this part for you. Be kind to yourself and watch what a difference it can make when you stop blaming yourself or beating yourself up, thinking that you are not worth the trouble.

The Magic of Putting Yourself First

Self-care is not selfish. Let that thought become ingrained in your mind. When you put yourself first, you will have so much more to give to yourself, your goal, your career, and the people around you. Every facet of your life will seem to blossom and grow when you take the time to prioritize yourself. When you practice self-care, this is what happens:

- **You Become Someone Who Gives More** - It's harder for you to offer your help to other people when you're not in a good place yourself. Life can be stressful. That's the world that we live in today. It's face-paced, it's on the move, it changes every minute, and we have to balance more on our plate these days than we had to several years ago. Personal life, family, work, relationships, friendships, financial responsibilities, other responsibilities. It's a lot to handle, and if we don't proactively take steps to take care of ourselves, the pressure can easily get to us. If you're feeling stressed and overwhelmed, there is no way you're going to be focused or strong enough to help anyone else. It is going to feel like a *huge* effort to help anyone else when it feels like you need help too. If you're someone who loves to lend a helping hand, this is going to make you feel guilty, and that guilt is only going to make you even more stressed than you already are. Guilt is not the best emotion to carry around with you when you're trying to work on building your confidence.

- **Your Happiness Is Going to Be Contagious** - When you're happy, it is going to show. The people who spend the most time with you are going to see and feel your happiness. Even a smile is going to go a long way when you're feeling buoyant and confident. A happy and positive attitude is always going to transcend and overflow into the other areas of your life. Other people love being around people who are happy and confident, and when you embody both these qualities because you're taking care of yourself and your needs, you're going to attract more good people into your life. They're going to be drawn to you and your infectious happiness. Self-care reminds you that there are good things to look forward to in your life, something to feel happy and positive about. If you are going to maintain the motivation you need to keep going, it is very important that you find ways to stay positive, no matter what obstacles you may face. When you take time to take care of yourself and destress, everything else in your life will fall into place.

- **You're Going to Become A Lot More Grateful and Motivated** - Positive energy in your life goes a long way. It keeps you motivated, passionate about your life, enthusiastic, and grateful. Self-care teaches you to count your blessings more and to be grateful for all the little things you get to do. So often, we take for granted how good we have it in life. Eating three full meals a day. Going to a spa when we feel the need to unwind. Coming back to a comfortable home and relaxing in front of the TV at the end of a long day. There are people out there who don't even know where their next meal is coming from. They don't have the luxury of being able to spend money on certain self-care measures, even if they wanted to. Practicing self-care is an exercise that makes you actively think about the good things happening in your life. That despite the difficult day you might have had, there were still moments of positivity in it that brought a smile to your face. Taking the time to count your blessings is one approach to achieving more balance in your life. It's hard to be negative and grateful at the same time. When you're a lot more relaxed and happy, you become a lot more motivated to reach your goals. When other people see how motivated you've become to reach your goals, you just might be the inspiration they need that pushes them to go after what they want in life too.

- **You're Going to Become More Understanding** - Self-care will make you a lot more compassionate towards yourself and the people around you. The guilt is going to eventually fade away when you begin to understand the importance of self-care. You've heard of the term *"The straw that breaks the camel's back."* The straw keeps getting piled onto the camel until one day, a little piece of straw is enough to bring the entire pile crumbling down. That is what happens when you don't take the time to look after yourself. In any self-improvement journey, including one where you're learning to say "no" to others, you're going to make mistakes along the way. If you don't learn to forgive yourself for the mistakes, setbacks, and disappointments, you're not going to make any kind of positive progress in cultivating that mindset for success. Developing compassion for yourself gives you the opportunity to build the kind of mindset where you're focused on learning from your mistakes, rather than beating yourself up for it. You don't have to be perfect all the time, and you don't need to try and do it all. Trying to do too much without balancing it out by looking after yourself is going to be the straw that breaks in the camel's back.

- **You're Calmer** - When you're stressed, every little thing is going to set you off. The simplest things can trigger a lot of stress these days. Running late, getting stuck in traffic, getting an unexpected text message with less than thrilling news, your boss asking you to take on an extra assignment at the last minute when you're already rushing to meet a deadline. It's unfortunate that we experience stress, so often we don't even know the difference anymore. We've come to accept being stressed out as the new norm. It's even possible to feel stressed out at home these days. Maybe you felt stressed when you had to pay the bills earlier or while you were watching the news. Perhaps scrolling through social media made you feel stressed seeing pictures of your happy friends when your life feels like it's in chaos. When a friend texts you for a favor and you're reluctant to say yes because you would rather be relaxing at home. Life can quickly start to feel like it's becoming too much to handle when you're not looking after your mental, physical, and emotional wellbeing on top of everything else.

- **You're Not Going to Be Burned Out** - Nothing is going to stop you dead in your tracks like burnout. When you're burned out, *nothing can get done.* We don't take burnout quite as seriously as we should. Only when it happens, do we wake up and realize that something needs to be done. Only then do we realize that if things don't change, it is never going to get better. The problem with burnout is that it can happen with no warning. You're pushing, pushing, pushing, and then suddenly, everything feels like it's too much once you hit your limit. You won't see the burnout coming, and when it hits, it is going to hit you like a ton of bricks. Self-care is the only way to avoid that. When you need help, ask for it. It can be one of the strongest things that you do for yourself. Avoid the negative consequences of burnout *before* it happens by proactively looking after yourself.

Self-Care Tips to Becoming a More Confident Person

We live in stressful and sometimes crazy times. If we don't take the time to look after ourselves, it can really mess with our minds. The little things that you do for yourself can go a long way toward making a big difference in your life.

- **Cut Toxic People Out of Your Life** - This is probably the most important self-care thing you can do. Toxic people do nothing but breed negativity and bad vibes. Toxic relationships can quickly bring you down, and if you constantly let your emotions get in the way of your actions, you could be that toxic relationship. A damaged relationship is not always easy to repair, and to avoid damaging it at all in the first place; you need to always make it a habit to cut toxic people out of your life once and for all. Toxic personalities are only going to create more unnecessary drama in your life. This is the unforeseen toxicity, one that is going to leave you feeling miserable because toxic personalities are nothing more than a drain on your energy. Toxic personalities will never be truly happy, no matter what you do for them. There will always be a reason to complain, a reason why it is never good enough. They will hold you back and weigh you down in life, diminishing your confidence and belief in yourself. It can be difficult to leave once you've formed a bond with them, especially if you care about them. None of the confidence or self-esteem tips you've learned so far are going to be of any use to you if you still keep these toxic people around. They'll unravel any good that you do to try and boost your confidence. Cut them out and toss them out. You don't have to be their enemy, but you don't have to be their friend either. If you can't cut them out of your life completely for one reason or another, then the next best thing to do is to limit your contact with them. With toxic people, you need to have high standards. If someone is not treating you the way you deserve or value what you have to offer, then they're not suited to be in your life. It is as simple as that.
- **Keep A Journal** - This can have a huge impact on your emotional and mental wellbeing. Journals have served as an outlet for their owners to record all the personal emotions, ideas, thoughts, reflections, views, experiences, and more by allowing them to privately document their thoughts in a "safe space," so to speak. That safe space is a journal that is meant for their eyes alone, and they can rest assured that no one else will be able to

read their innermost thoughts unless they want them to. Journaling is a great way to help keep you on the right track towards being more mindful. You know that sense of relief that you get when you've successfully let your emotions out? That feeling that you get when you've confided in someone about everything that is bothering you and you feel as if a huge weight has been lifted off your shoulders? That's the same kind of effect that you get with journaling. Journaling promotes a state of mindfulness because when you're writing down all that you are feeling, you are acknowledging your thoughts and paying attention to them, really seeing them down on paper for the first time in a way you may not otherwise be able to if they are all just jumbled up in your mind. Instead of letting your mind wander, and your thoughts get out of control, writing them down in a response journal will force you to bring them into focus, especially when you ask yourself questions in the journal and then attempt to answer them.

- **Be Selfish With Your Time** - Your time is precious, and you should invest time in the things you want to do. Everyone deserves some alone time to recuperate, and if you feel that you need some time to yourself, take it. Take as much time off as you need, and don't let anyone make you feel bad about it. To avoid being overwhelmed, you must be selfishly protective of your time. If you don't, other people will always have more control over you than they should. They'll keep asking you for favors too if they know that you're not going to say no to them. Be selfish with your time. Spend it with yourself when you need to. Spend more time with people who bring out the best in you instead. You are not obligated to spend more time with the toxic person than you should. You're not obligated to keep saying yes and doing things for other people at the risk of neglecting your own needs. Don't feel about being selfishly protective of your time. This is something that must be done for the sake of your emotional wellbeing. Your quiet time is not something you should willingly compromise on. This is part of your self-care process and a way to balance your mental and physical wellbeing. Your quiet time routine can be anything that works for you. Go for a walk, stretch your muscles, spend time alone until you feel better, taking short breaks throughout the day to step away from people. Retreating to your quiet time is the easiest way to keep yourself from feeling emotionally exhausted, and quiet time can be done anywhere, and whenever you feel it.
- **Take A Step Back from Social Media** - Social media is fun, but it can also be a very toxic place to spend too much time in. Social media has a way of drawing us in and keeping us hooked

for hours, but it isn't as relaxing as we think. When your mind is still absorbing some of the negativity you see on social media, that is not taking care of yourself. Unplugging from the media is essential to avoid overwhelming your senses. It's good to take a step back every now and then from the negativity, shock value, sensationalism, and extremely traumatic or emotional moments that certain content on social platforms can expose you to. None of which are good if they're overloading your senses. It doesn't help that we all have minds that are biased toward being attracted to the negative in the first place. Continuously feeding your mind with this type of content is only going to make it harder for you to find peace and balance, so avoid it whenever you can and choose to spend some quiet time alone instead. This is an outstanding self-care and survival practice that is going to help you thrive without feeling overwhelmed.

- **Set Boundaries** - Set boundaries because you need them. Without boundaries, people are always going to take advantage of you, even if they don't realize that they're doing it. Without boundaries, you're always going to have a hard time saying no to requests. Without boundaries, there can be no self-care. Healthy boundaries are your ultimate protection against being too overwhelmed. Protecting yourself and your own self-worth comes first, and you should never allow yourself to be emotionally bullied by anyone, no matter who they are. Do not let someone else make you feel that you are unworthy or inferior; this kind of behavior pattern is dangerous. Setting boundaries helps to protect yourself from them because it helps to limit how much influence they will have over your life. Setting boundaries can be in the form of limiting your time with them or finding a support system to help you manage your emotions after each encounter. It would depend on the situation you may be in. By defining your boundaries, you will come to understand what your limits are, and this will make it much easier for you to say no in favor of looking after yourself.
- **Exercise and Eat Right** - Sometimes, the simplest solutions can turn out to be the most effective. Physical exercise is the best relaxation technique out there for both your mind and body that won't cost you a thing. Your lifestyle habits play a big part in the current state of your stress levels. It is recommended that you exercise at least three to four times a week for 30-minutes per session. Perform moderate to intense exercises like jogging, brisk walking, cycling, hiking, or any form of aerobic activity that is going to get your heart rate up. This gives your endorphin levels a boost, a hormone that helps you feel good and feel happy. The perfect antidote to combat stress. Don't forget to eat well too. The

stress of everyday pressures may have had a disruptive effect on your eating patterns. Now that you are taking a more proactive role in your self-care routine, you can start making an effort to eat well again. Keep your mind sharp, and your body fit by eating a well- balanced diet that meets all their nutritional needs and steers clear of anything that is going to impact your body in a negative way. Take it a step further by combining it with an exercise routine too. Living a healthy lifestyle can do wonders for your mental and emotional health. You're going to start feeling really good about yourself because you like the results that you see in the mirror. When you know that you look good, you start to feel good. You're energetic, you're clear-minded, you feel good, and you feel like you are ready to take on any challenge that is thrust at you. You become a more confident person, and this is going to give your ability to say no a huge boost when you've got the confidence you need to back you up.

CONCLUSION

Thank you for making it through to the end of *Self-Confidence for Beginners*, let's hope it was informative and able to provide you with all of the tools you need to achieve your goals, whatever they may be.

You are an incredible person, and you have a lot to offer the world. Once you embrace this, it becomes so much easier to start building that confidence from within. Start building your confidence from within, and it will shine through externally. Confidence is going to be the difference as to whether you enjoy your life or live miserably. Now that you know the steps that must be taken to start working on building your confidence, the rest is up to you from this point forward. What is life if you don't enjoy it, right?

Choose today to be a positive person. With hard work, determination, and the right attitude, you can make all the steps in this book work for you. The confidence that you display in your life is going to change everything. It's going to show in your job, your relationships, even your finances. If you make the commitment to be confident, you're going to see results very quickly.

Finally, if you found this book useful in any way, a review on Amazon is always appreciated!

DESCRIPTION

To all the self-confidence seekers out there, you are not alone.
Life can seem significantly harder when you don't have confidence on your side. Confidence is something that you have to teach yourself over time. The only way to become the best version of yourself is through hard work, and that is what this process is. *Hard work,* but it is hard work that is going to be worth it when you see what a difference confidence makes in your life.

Confidence is something that is bigger than you. It is an unseen force that motivates you, supports you, pushes you to become the very best that you can be. It gives you the courage you need to face any challenge that comes your way. It strengthens your belief that you are good enough and worthy enough to achieve anything that you want in life. It lets you know that it is okay to fail because you have the strength and the resilience you need to pick yourself up again. It teaches you to recognize the opportunities that come into your life and gives you the courage to seize the moment before it slips through your fingers.

That is just a snippet of what a difference confidence can make in your life. Is it an easy skill to cultivate? Not all the time. Is it going to be worth it? Absolutely! Confidence is not something you're born with. It's a skillset. This is a skill set that you are about to learn in this book. *Self-Confidence* is packed with all the essential tips you need to get over those mental and emotional hurdles that have been holding you back in life for far too long.

Confidence is a journey that starts from within. It has to begin with a strong desire to be the change you want to see in your life. Nobody else can do it for you, and the good news is, you've already taken a step in the right direction when you stumbled upon this book. *Self-Confidence* will expose you to:

- How to drop your old mindset and begin to understand what confidence truly means.
- How to take the necessary steps to move out of your comfort zone.
- Why you need to expose yourself to challenges to grow.
- What you can do to effectively deal with your nervous anxiety because anxiety and confidence cannot exist side by side.
- Who your inner critic is, what it does, and how you can stomp it out for good, so it never holds you back again.
- Why tough personalities and characters are the ones that turn out to be the most confident of all.
- Why self-care is not selfish, and why you should never let anyone make you feel bad for taking the time you need to look after yourself.

Confidence truly is the key that makes a remarkable difference in your life. If you believe in yourself, the whole world will believe in you too. Perception is reality, and the secret to getting ahead in life is, really, no big secret at all. It's merely confidence. Are you ready to become a happier, fulfilled, confident person? Let's get right to it.

www.ingramcontent.com/pod-product-compliance
Lightning Source LLC
Chambersburg PA
CBHW071456070526
44578CB00001B/358